JOURNEY WITHOUT A DESTINATION

Is there a solution for Sri Lankan refugees?

Rohini Hensman

Contents

Foreword

Rohini Hensman's Journey without a Destination is the story of Sri Lanka's bloody civil war, told in the words of those displaced or dispossessed by the fighting.

Over half a million Sri Lankan Tamil refugees have fled to other countries while over a million Sri Lankans are displaced internally by the continuing conflict.

Her in-depth interviews bear witness to the complexities and the contradictions of a society at war with itself – the conflicting emotions of those who have fled the country, the hopes and fears of those who are internal refugees.

She charts in the process an incisive oral history of Tamil and Sinhalese nationalism – two cultures on a collision course – and a human cost that can never be adequately measured.

She has found that those who suffer sometimes have insights that could hasten a solution – insights inevitably based on tolerance and understanding.

These are qualities that we also urgently need in European countries if we are to face up to our own responsibilities – to help and support those who seek refuge from such savage conflicts.

Alf Dubs, Director
British Refugee Council
[1993]

Preface

It seems almost banal to say that when you set out on a journey, it is with a destination in mind: why would you set out otherwise? Yet millions of people embark on a desperate journey without any destination, impelled only by the desire to escape from the horror behind them, or forcibly driven from their homes. These are the refugees of the world; and Sri Lanka, considering how small it is, has made a sizeable contribution to their numbers.

Technically, only those who escape to another country are called 'refugees', while those who remain in their own country are called 'displaced persons'. However, I refer to both groups as 'refugees' in this book in order to emphasise the essential similarity of their experience.

Recently, a great deal of hostility to refugees has been expressed in Britain and other Western countries. One example is John Major's statement, 'We must not be wide open to all comers just because Rome, Paris and London are more attractive than Bombay or Algiers' (*The Independent* 2/7/91, p. 6). Yet the overwhelming bulk of Third World refugees flee to other Third World countries; in the case of Sri Lanka too, the number who flee to India is many times greater than the number who go to all the other countries of the world put together: 250,000 in India in 1991, compared with 80,000 in the West (see also Kismaric 1989, p. 119). But perhaps this is only due to lack of opportunity? Is it possible that all those teeming millions out there are just waiting to flock to Britain and other Western countries, and that the label 'refugees' is just a convenient excuse?

This is one of the questions that I set out to answer in the project which initiated this book, begun in 1989. I have taken Sri Lanka as a paradigm of the countries from which refugees are fleeing, and Britain as a paradigm of the Western countries in which they seek asylum.

Although both countries of course have their own peculiarities, I believe that – paradoxical though it may seem – it is possible to learn more about the fate and treatment of refugees in general from an in-depth study of this kind than from a more cursory examination of a variety of situations, although such studies are useful in their own way. There is also a point in confining the study to refugees and not taking up the more general question of immigration. Although refugees in the country where they seek asylum in many ways share the fate of immigrants, there is a fundamental difference in their situations. Immigrants, for a variety of reasons, wish to leave their homeland and settle in another country; refugees have no such wish, but are forced to leave their country as a result of political developments there. Successful settlement abroad cannot, therefore, be seen as a completely satisfactory permanent solution to the problem of refugees; in this they have more in common with displaced people who remain in their own country, because for both, the ideal solution is a situation where they can live in peace in their own homes.

Thus the responsibility of the international community towards refugees does not end with the provision of decent conditions of asylum, although this is of course essential. There is also an international responsibility to do whatever is possible to end the crisis which has driven them out of their homes, and help them to return and rebuild their lives there if they wish to do so. To see the problem in its entirety, therefore, it is also necessary to look at what has caused the refugee outflow in the first place, and how this can be remedied.

To begin with, I carried out in-depth interviews with 53 Tamil refugees in Britain, asking why they had decided to leave Sri Lanka, and why they had chosen to come to Britain rather than any other country. A few said they had come to Britain temporarily as students, and had been stranded when the violence broke out; most had not wished to leave Sri Lanka at all until forced to do so. As one refugee put it: 'I didn't choose to go anywhere – I didn't want to go anywhere – I didn't decide to leave at all.'

Many had suffered loss of status and identity as a result of the move, and longed to go back, provided they could go back to a home and not to a war. They seem a very far cry from people who had wished to come to Britain in order to improve their prospects – so-called 'economic migrants' – even though only a very small minority of them had succeeded in getting full refugee status. As one refugee commented, 'The British government is saying the Tamils are economic refugees, but I don't agree with that – that is not true. I myself was the chief accountant in a government department; there were 64 people working under me. If the Tamils fleeing from there are all economic refugees, why should the doctors, engineers and accountants come?'

Why indeed? As this comment suggests, I found that virtually all the refugees I interviewed in Britain had been well-educated and came from a fairly affluent background in Sri Lanka: many were doctors, lawyers, accountants, technicians, engineers, senior government officials, teachers, lecturers, etc. Some of the women had not been employed, but all except the very oldest had been educated up to 'O' level or beyond. Some had difficulties with English, but many others spoke it fluently. Their ages ranged from 18 to 70; some had been students, and a few were continuing their studies in Britain. I gathered that, before they were affected by the conflict, they had been comfortable or even well off in Sri Lanka.

Of course, they could all have been lying; they could have made up elaborate stories to deceive me and the immigration authorities. One way of checking up on them was to look through documentary accounts of the situation they claimed to be describing; another was to visit Sri Lanka and see for myself.

I did both, doing extensive background reading and visiting Sri Lanka twice, in 1990 and 1991. The documentary sources agreed remarkably well with the refugees' accounts; and I found Sri Lanka full of displaced people, the number increasing from around 1 million during the first visit to around 1.6 or 1.7 million during the second – more than one-tenth of the island's entire population. If we are to discount the stories of the refugees in Britain as being untrue, we would also have to dismiss the documented accounts, including those by reputable organisations like Amnesty International, as being mistaken; and we would have to believe that all the people herded into refugee camps throughout Sri Lanka in wretched conditions were there for a picnic.

Somehow, it doesn't seem likely. Maybe people who make allegations about bogus asylum claims would change their minds if they went through the same enquiries as I did. Indeed, it is a good deal easier to prescribe that others should live in constant danger than to do so oneself. Some refugees felt that officials should see the situation for themselves before making judgements.

But why had the refugees chosen to come to Britain? Some had not chosen to, but had landed up in Britain more or less by chance. Those who had made the decision had done so mainly for one or more of three reasons: (1) because they already had relatives settled in Britain; (2) because they had a knowledge of English; (3) because up to the end of May 1985, there was an open visa system for all Commonwealth citizens.

As one refugee explained, when asked why he had chosen to come to Britain: 'It's the only country we can come to because we are Commonwealth citizens and no visas were required at that time. So we had to flee to a country where the language that we speak is spoken, and in fact I had my daughter here then. She's settled down – she's a British citizen. It was at her request that I came here.'

All three reasons are related to a fact which too often seems to be ignored: namely, that colonials in London and Paris were attracted to Bombay and Algiers long before the reverse flow started; and that the British were in Sri Lanka for a century and a half not merely as uninvited guests but as unwanted rulers who deprived its people of their rights in their own country. Against this background, the air of injured innocence of the Western powers rings rather hollow. It is worth looking at allegations by some refugees that, both historically and currently, Britain bears part of the responsibility for the crisis that is displacing millions of Sri Lankans.

It is all the more urgent to put the record straight because irresponsible untruths in high places cost lives. The situation in Britain today is such that the lives of refugees seeking asylum are at risk not merely from forcible repatriation but also from more direct physical attacks. On 29 December 1991 a Sri Lankan refugee, Panchadcharam Sahitharan, was assaulted by racist thugs in East London, and died four days later without regaining consciousness. He was not the first refugee to be killed by British racists. It is a tragic irony that refugees fleeing ethnic violence in their own countries should face exactly the same problem in the countries where they seek asylum. Anyone who fosters the myth that refugees are scroungers is condoning a society which tolerates these murders.

It has often been pointed out that, on the contrary, refugees are a resource for the country where they seek asylum. The majority of Sri Lankan refugees in Britain are highly skilled, educated, qualified people who could contribute a great deal to Britain if they were allowed to do so.

In fact, the country which suffers from the 'problem' of Sri Lankan refugees is Sri Lanka itself. The exodus of so many skilled and qualified people, the killing of many more, and the disruption of education, has put the development process back many decades. And, of course, it is a problem for the refugees themselves, who do not wish to go anywhere and only want to live and work in peace in their own country. Is there any prospect that they could do this in the foreseeable future?

The predominant picture of Sri Lanka as a country locked in irreconcilable ethnic conflict suggests that the answer is 'no'. However, my own personal starting point for this project was a childhood memory which didn't quite fit in with this picture. My family had lived in a Sinhala-speaking suburb of Colombo without ever feeling any hostility from our neighbours. When anti-Tamil riots broke out in 1958, Sinhalese friends who suspected that an attack on us was being planned not only warned us, but spared no effort to ensure that we escaped to safety, with the help of many others. What stands out in my memory is the love and concern of our Sinhalese friends and neighbours, who on that occasion probably saved our lives.

Could this be a mistake, or perhaps a unique experience? In order to find out, I asked the refugees about their own relationships with friends, colleagues and neighbours from other ethnic groups. Most of them spoke with warmth and affection of such relationships, and there were numerous instances where help had been given; many could, like me, recall living peacefully in multi-ethnic communities. What, then, had caused the problem, and were there any possible solutions?

A very wide range of opinions was expressed in response to these questions. A few tend to confirm the view that there is no meeting point, and therefore no solution. But the majority are impressively clear-sighted and humane – so much more so than the views expressed by most political leaders in Sri Lanka, that it made me think of these refugees as not mere victims of the violence, but as people well able to contribute to a solution.

It is all too easy to see refugees as objects – objects of violence in the first place, and then objects of relief and rehabilitation. Even if attempts are made to satisfy their special needs, this still doesn't amount to seeing them as intelligent human beings. The first requirement is that we should listen to them, and that, really, is the purpose of this book. What they have to say about the situation in Sri Lanka is valuable because it shows what can be done by Sri Lankans, as well as by the international community, to put an end to the violence. Their wisdom comes from suffering, and they were generous enough to share it with me: I in turn would like to share it with others in the hope that it will help to put an end to their suffering.

Where there are gaps in my narrative, I fill them from documentary sources, and also include a bibliography of such sources at the end. But most of the story is told in the words of the refugees themselves; it is their experiences and insights which make this account distinctive. On the other hand, we have to recognise that many of them, and in some cases their relatives, are in an extremely vulnerable position, which could be made worse by unwelcome publicity. In attempting to protect their identities, I did not even ask for names and addresses, and have tried to give them the voice which they so desperately need without inviting the reprisals that are so often the punishment for speaking out. It is not possible to find a solution to the problem of Sri Lankan refugees so long as the people most affected are gagged by terror.

The refugees interviewed in Britain in 1989 were all Tamil, and Chapters 1, 2 and 3 are based on what they said. Chapter 4 is about Tamil refugees within Sri Lanka, Chapters 5 and 6, which deal with the idea of a Sinhalese and a Tamil state respectively, take up the experience of Sinhalese and Muslim refugees in Sri Lanka; and Chapter 7 is based on positive solutions proposed by all these groups. The predominance of Tamils is due to the fact that the Tamil refugee problem has been going on for much longer than the others; and it is also the case that whereas there are parts of Sri Lanka which are relatively safe for people of other communities, there is no part of Sri Lanka where Tamils are safe.

Major political changes took place between the interviews in Britain in 1989 and my visits to the camps in Sri Lanka in October 1990 and September 1991. In June-July 1989 the Indian army was still in Sri Lanka: having entered in 1987 as a peace-keeping force it had by then become embroiled in a war with the Liberation Tigers of Tamil Eelam (LTTE) in which Tamil civilians were once more the victims; the uprising of the Janatha Vimukthi Peramuna (JVP – a Sinhalese militant group) and its repression by the Sri Lankan government were in full spate; and there was a ceasefire between the Sri Lankan government and the LTTE, the most powerful of the Tamil militant groups (see Chronology).

By the time I visited Sri Lanka in 1990, the Indian army had left, the JVP uprising had been all but crushed, and the ceasefire between the government and the LTTE had broken down; moreover, the LTTE was for the first time carrying out open attacks on Muslim civilians. Thus, the circumstances which had led to the flight of the displaced people in Sri Lanka were in most cases different from those recounted by the refugees in Britain, although there were some events in common.

Where not otherwise indicated, I have put my questions and comments to refugees in bold italics. Bullet points indicate the beginning of quotations from the testimony of refugees. I have made a few small changes to the original in the interests of clarity and convenience; for example, where references to University Teachers for Human Rights (Jaffna) reports were to the hard copies, I have changed them to online references, with links in the Bibliography.

Acknowledgements

I would like to thank the Nuffield Foundation and the Refugee Studies Programme, Christian Aid and the World Council of Churches for funding the research for and writing of this book; the British Refugee Council, Tamil Refugee Action Group and South London Tamil Welfare Group for helping to organise the interviews in Britain; Sr. Angela, Sr. Martha, Sr. Antonita and Sr. Jayanthi, Anberia, Faizun and Yasmine, Scholastica, Lenita and Rajani for helping to organise the visits to refugee camps in Sri Lanka; and the staff at Satyodaya for helping me to meet refugees in the plantation areas and victims of the Janatha Vimukthi Peramuna (JVP) conflict. My thanks also to Carol and Tim for so generously providing housing for my family while I was working on the book. Above all I would like to thank the refugees who talked to me for taking the time to tell me about their experiences and ideas; this book is dedicated to them, in the hope that the future will heal the wounds of their past.

The British Refugee Council wishes to acknowledge the support and assistance of Christian Aid in making the publication of this book possible.

Rohini Hensman, Summer 1993

Postscript

Coming back to this text so many years later, I have to say one thing that I failed to say in the original Preface: neither in conducting the interviews nor in writing the book did I make any pretence at being 'neutral'. I made it clear to the refugees that my aim was to find a solution to the root problems in Sri Lanka that were creating the refugee crisis, and I should make that clear to readers of this account too.

At the time this book was written, Sri Lankan Tamils constituted a significant proportion of refugees worldwide. At present, although there are still many displaced people in Sri Lanka and the persecution of minorities as well as an extremely authoritarian state still plague the country (Hensman 2019), Sri Lankan refugees have been outnumbered by refugees from other countries. However, I feel the method of investigation and observations I have made in this book are as relevant to the current refugees, namely:

(1) Campaigning for humane asylum policies is undoubtedly important, but it is equally important to do whatever can be done to end the violence from which refugees are fleeing.

(2) It is crucially important to understand the complexities of the situation from which the refugees are fleeing. In Sri Lanka, for example, while atrocities by the Sinhala nationalist state were the prime reason for the exodus, Tamil nationalist militant groups, especially the LTTE, played a major role in reinforcing state violence and independently inflicting violence on Tamils, thus becoming a secondary reason for their flight; holding one actor responsible while glossing over the contribution of the other would, over the course of the next several years, achieve nothing. There are many such situations in the world today, where refugees are fleeing violence to which multiple actors are contributing, and simply condemning one side cannot solve the problem.

(3) Listening to what refugees and displaced persons have to say – about their experiences as well as their opinions about the conflict and possible solutions to it – is vital. On their experiences, *they* are the experts: no one else knows better than they do what they have been through and are going through. These experiences have to be part of any coherent account of the conflict. On explanations for the conflict and possible solutions, their opinions may vary; yet, as I found, a great deal of wisdom can be gleaned from their responses when their differing relationships to the various actors is taken into account, and any viable solution must take their viewpoints seriously. This point is particularly important today, when 'experts' often pontificate about conflicts while denying any voice to the actual victims, resulting in over-simplification and sometimes outright misrepresentation of the situation. Even people who call themselves socialists are guilty of doing this, blaming only their own *bête noir* while disregarding mass murder committed by tyrants supposedly opposed to their prime enemy. This book illustrates vividly why such a policy is not just a shameful refusal of

solidarity with some of the victims of oppression, but also contributes to the continuation of violence and war.

Rohini Hensman, January 2022.

Chronology of Major Events

1798-1948: British colonial rule in Ceylon (Sri Lanka).

1931: State-aided colonisation schemes to settle Sinhalese in the predominantly Tamil areas of the dry zone begun by D. S. Senanayake, then Minister of Agriculture and later the first Prime Minister after Independence.

1948: Independence. Newly-elected United National Party (UNP) government enacts Citizenship Act, making resident Tamils of Indian origin (Hill-country Tamils) into stateless persons.

1949: Indian and Pakistani Residents (Citizenship) Act makes registration dependent on the birth in Sri Lanka of ancestors, thus excluding 95% of Hill-country Tamils; Ceylon (Parliamentary) Election Amendment Act deprives Hill-country Tamils of voting rights.

1956: The Sri Lanka Freedom Party (SLFP) comes to power and enacts the Official Language Act, making Sinhala the only official language.

1957: The Bandaranaike-Chelvanayakam Pact recognises the use of Tamil in the North and East and regional devolution of power, but is then abrogated by the government.

1958: Non-violent protests by Tamils start. Island-wide anti-Tamil riots leave hundreds of Tamils dead; over 10,000 Tamil refugees taken from Colombo to Jaffna.

1959: SWRD Bandaranaike is assassinated by a Buddhist monk organisation angry about his attempts to meet Tamil demands.

1964: Pact between PM Sirimavo Bandaranaike and Indian PM Shastri agreeing that around 525,000 Hill-country Tamils would be repatriated to India and 300,000 given Sri Lankan citizenship.

1971: Uprising by Janatha Vimukthi Peramuna (JVP) rapidly put down by the government. SLFP government introduces 'standardisation' scheme which makes university entrance dependent not on merit but on quotas; the proportion of Tamil entrants falls as a result.

1972: New constitution gives Sinhala constitutional status as the only official language, and Buddhism the foremost place among religions, omitting guarantees of minority rights.

1972–1975: Nationalisation of plantations, accompanied by evictions of and violence against Hill-country Tamils, creating more refugees.

1974: Fourth World Tamil Research Conference in Jaffna attacked by Sinhalese police; 9 Tamils killed, hundreds injured.

1976: Tamil United Liberation Front (TULF) adopts Vaddukoddai Resolution calling for a separate Tamil state in the North and East; Tamil militant groups begin armed struggle to achieve it.

1977: Election victory of UNP followed by large-scale anti-Tamil riots creating over 50,000 Tamil refugees.

1978: J. R. Jayawardene introduces new Constitution confirming privileged status of Sinhala and Buddhism and making himself executive president with enormous powers.

1979: Prevention of Terrorism Act (PTA) passed allowing for incommunicado detention of suspects up to 18 months without their being brought before a magistrate; no judicial remedies for arbitrary detention, torture or extra-judicial execution.

1981: Island-wide anti-Tamil riots create more refugees. Jaffna Public Library, containing over 90,000 volumes including ancient Tamil manuscripts, reduced to ashes.

1982: Referendum, conducted amidst allegations of fraud and intimidation, results in cancellation of forthcoming parliamentary elections.

1983: Tamil militants ambush army, killing 13 soldiers; island-wide state-sponsored anti-Tamil violence in which thousands of Tamil civilians are killed, tens of thousands displaced.

1987: Signing of Indo-Sri Lanka Peace Accord in July, and entry of the Indian Peace-Keeping Force (IPKF) in accordance with its terms. In October, war breaks out between IPKF and Liberation Tigers of Tamil Eelam (LTTE), the most powerful of the Tamil militant groups. JVP launches insurrection. Government counter-insurgency measures include large-scale extra-judicial executions and reprisals against Sinhalese civilians.

1989: Negotiations between Sri Lankan government and LTTE begin in April, ceasefire announced in June. JVP leaders killed by security forces in November.

1990: IPKF leaves in March. LTTE massacres Sinhalese and Muslim policemen in June; ceasefire breaks down. In October, LTTE expels all Muslims from the North.

1990–1991: Attacks by security forces and Muslim Home Guards on Tamil civilians and by LTTE on Sinhalese and Muslim civilians leads to thousands of deaths and massive displacement.

Chapter 1: Understanding the refugee problem

How did it all start? What are the roots of the conflict which has led to such a massive exodus of people from their homes?

Only one of the refugees I met felt that the conflict pre-dated British rule, or had its roots in pre-colonial ethnic incompatibilities:

> • If anybody tells me that this conflict between the Sinhalese and Tamils is hardly 40 or 50 years old, then I would say that person is a liar. If the Mahavamsa and Culavamsa [Sinhalese epics] are anything to go by, our enmity dates back to the pre-Christian era during the time of Dutugemunu.

The overwhelming majority of the refugees, however, blamed the policies of successive Sri Lankan governments. For example:

> • It's the government. I don't blame individuals – the people are really good. We still have good Sinhalese friends. Many of these friends write to us, still. And even after the troubles, it was my husband's friends who sponsored our passports, because they have to sign a bond.

Sinhalese friends?

> Yes. Tamil friends didn't want to do it at that time, because all were scared and thought they might leave the country, so they didn't want to commit too much. So our Sinhalese friends did it. Individually, they are very nice people. But the government is making use of the uneducated crowd. I never get angry with any Sinhalese person.

Which of these two views is more plausible? It is true that there is evidence for conflict between Sinhalese and Tamil kings; but these could be seen as expressions of political rivalry rather than ethnic incompatibility. What is remarkable, indeed, is the degree to which Sinhalese- and Tamil-speaking communities influenced each other, mingled, and even inter-married, in pre-colonial times (Bandaranayake 1984).

One or two refugees felt that the basis for future strife had been laid by British colonial policies:

> • I think all the trouble was created by the British, because Sri Lanka is a former colony of Britain… When they left the country – when they gave us so-called 'independence' – they gave power to the

Sinhalese, the Buddhist monks, who started to destroy our Tamil identities.

This charge is difficult to evaluate. The constitution at Independence did contain safeguards for minorities that were later removed (Hyndman 1988), but it also left the possibility that the Sinhalese majority could abuse its position of power. My own feeling is that British rule was more destructive in the way that it distorted the Sri Lankan economy for its own benefit, laying the basis for future poverty and underdevelopment, and creating the possibility that a struggle for resources could take the form of ethnic strife.

The charge that the problem has been caused by the Sri Lankan government was substantiated by reference to specific policies, beginning with the first United National Party (UNP) government, which in the year of independence passed an Act which excluded the vast majority of Hill-country Tamils from franchise and citizenship. As one refugee said:

• In 1948, when the Citizenship Act was brought in, my family became stateless. Then in the 1950s my father made an application under the Citizenship Act, and was one of the very few people who got citizenship under the Citizenship Act. Then, of course, there have been other agreements with the Indian government for repatriation and all that – this is one type of discrimination.

Tamil-speaking people in Sri Lanka constitute more than one ethnic community. Most Hill-country Tamils, or Tamils of recent Indian origin, came or were brought to Sri Lanka from India as plantation or estate workers during British rule, and thus became vulnerable to this specific form of discrimination, which deprived them of their franchise and citizenship; later, when the plantations were nationalised in 1972 and 1975, many of them were driven off the plantations to become displaced people, and in some cases to starve.

Tamil-speaking Muslims (or Moors) are another distinct ethnic group; and even the Sri Lanka Tamils, who are the largest group, sometimes identify themselves by the area of their origin, especially in the case of Jaffna Tamils.

Other policies which were seen to have led to the conflict were: (1) the Official Language Act of 1956, often known as the 'Sinhala Only Act' because it made Sinhala the only official language; (2) the resulting discrimination against Tamil speakers, especially in government employment; and (3) the 'standardisation' and 'district quota' systems in higher education, which were supposed to help educationally deprived sections to get university places, but actually resulted in discrimination against Tamils (Hyndman 1988).

The colonisation policies of successive governments, which were aimed at altering the population distribution by settling Sinhalese in predominantly Tamil areas, also caused enormous resentment. Last but not least, pogroms against Tamils, seen to have been carried out with government instigation – in terms of propaganda as well as organisation – were for many people the last straw. Groups seen as having a powerful influence, especially the Buddhist monks and the media, were also blamed. With few exceptions, the Tamil refugees felt that without these provocations the separatist movement would never have arisen.

In the wake of the massacre of Tamils in the 1983 riots, the UNP government reacted by outlawing the Tamil members of the Tamil United Liberation Front (TULF) who were demanding a separate state by non-violent means. Some Tamils felt then that all legal, peaceful methods of obtaining their rights had been tried and had failed. The militant movement, already engaged in an armed struggle for a Tamil state which had begun in the mid-1970s, began to receive much more widespread support, the militants becoming popularly known as 'the boys'.

The legislation of 1948 and 1949, which deprived the hill-country Tamils of their citizenship and franchise, led to protests in parliament but no open violence; it was only in the 1960s, when deportation of those who were not granted Sri Lanka citizenship began, that thousands of people arrived in India as refugees.

By contrast, the 'Sinhala Only' policy followed by SWRD Bandaranaike's SLFP government from 1956 onwards resulted in non-violent protests from Tamils, which in turn led to major rioting in 1958, as some of the refugees recalled:

> • There was no problem before 1958 – it was only after that all this started. It was created by politicians for their own benefit and for their power.

As the refugees did not say much about this early period, I quote from an account by a prominent Sinhalese journalist and editor, Tarzie Vittachi, written soon after the events:

> Bandaranaike… enacted the Sinhalese Only Act, thereby setting off a series of disorders two months after the new government took over… The area most seriously affected was the Gal Oya Valley… [O]ver 150 people were killed during that brief spell of open race-hate… In August 1957 the Tamils threatened an island-wide

Satyagraha or civil disobedience campaign. This danger was averted by the forging of a pact between Bandaranaike and the Federal Party leader, Chelvanayakam. Almost exactly a year later the Bandaranaike-Chelvanayakam (or B-C) Pact was jettisoned, which led to the large-scale riots and bloodshed of May-June 1958. (Vittachi 1958, p. 20)

Attacks on Tamils by gangs of Sinhalese thugs began on 22 May: the hooligans acted with the apparent assurance that the government was on their side, and the Prime Minister seemed to confirm this assumption:

On Tuesday morning, 27 May, at 7.15, a group of citizens who had distinguished themselves in various fields of public activity called urgently to see the Prime Minister and implored him to proclaim a State of Emergency. Mr Bandaranaike's answer was that it was an 'exaggeration' to call the situation an 'emergency'. His supplicants later said they were appalled at the insouciance with which the Prime Minister appeared to be taking the mass murders, looting and lawlessness which had broken out everywhere. (Vittachi 1958, pp. 45–6)

Later that day, however, a State of Emergency was declared by the Governor-General, a dusk-to-dawn curfew was imposed, and the army and navy were called out to quell the violence. Although the arson and looting continued for several days, calm was gradually restored. By the second week of the Emergency,

the refugee population in Colombo had grown to formidable proportions: 12,000 men, women and children of every imaginable walk of life were herded together in temporary camps… (Vittachi 1958, p. 87)

The purpose of the rioters, as outlined in pamphlets sent to the government, was to 'clear Tamils out' of areas of Sri Lanka which they saw as being exclusively Sinhalese. As one pamphlet threatened:

Don't think that you or any of the Tamils will be safe, as we have enough petrol to make living torches of all of you and monuments of the Tamil houses… We have the priests behind us and every temple will come out into the open against you if you try to use force on us… Be warned. Death is at your doorstep. Act now and join us in our struggle for freedom from the Tamils and other aliens such as the Muslims, Malays, Burghers [Sri Lankans with some European ancestry], etc, all of whom can go to the Northern and Eastern Provinces if they want to remain in Sri Lanka… (Vittachi 1958)

Bandaranaike's weak attempts to restrain his followers led to his assassination by a fanatical Buddhist monk organisation in 1959. The violence abated, but the government policies which made Tamils feel like second-class citizens continued, laying the basis, as the Tamil refugees felt, for the present conflict. One said:

> • The basic reason was discrimination against Tamils in several things – getting jobs, higher studies – they didn't get a chance. I asked why this movement, these groups, started, and they said these are the reasons.

Another said:

> • Segregation, for a start. Segregation, denial of rights… the standardisation of education. Because Tamil citizens weren't given an equal opportunity to enter university. I know friends who got double the marks of Sinhalese friends in the same university, but still haven't been given the opportunity… one person had to come back and do petty jobs after doing his A levels. This is one of the main reasons why I had to join EROS [Eelam Revolutionary Organisation of Students, one of the militant groups].

Another explained it in terms of language and politics:

> • At the start, Tamil people were well educated in English, and they were having top-rank positions in government. Even in the minor clerical grades, there were Tamil people holding positions. But when Bandaranaike came in 1956, he thought the only way to change this was by changing the medium of instruction as well as the medium used in government offices to Sinhala. So then Tamil peoples were deprived, they had to start again from 'ayanah aayanah' [the ABC].
>   When they introduced swabasha (the vernacular) as the medium of instruction at university level, I liked it. We were going very fast; immediately they were asked to translate all the English books into Tamil and Sinhala. So Bandaranaike did something good for both communities, Tamil as well as Sinhalese. But there was discrimination. Tamil people had to study Sinhala, and even after studying Sinhala they were still discriminated against. I translated

Sinhala poems and other things into Tamil. But I lost my job after 17 years' service because they couldn't guarantee my security.

Do you think there would have been no conflict if not for that discrimination?

Definitely. If there was no language barrier, this conflict would not have arisen. Bandaranaike wanted to come to power, and the only weapon he had was this language weapon.

Other refugees agreed that the government's discrimination was the main cause of the conflict:

• The groups are fighting for the freedom of the Tamil community. The Tamil community and the Sinhala community are separate and they can't live happily, that's why. Earlier we were all together, but the government's attitude to Tamils and Sinhalese was totally different: in education, in work, there was government discrimination. Then we felt, if we're separate, we'll be happy. The government first made this problem; we were all happy with Sinhalese people before…

• Tamils are treated as secondary people, and the Sinhala leaders, or Sinhala government, are not willing to accept Tamils' self-determination. Earlier the Sinhala leaders and Tamil leaders signed an agreement – the Banda-Chelva agreement – but the government didn't implement it.

Do you think this problem would have arisen if the Bandaranaike-Chelvanayakam Pact had been honoured?

No! If the Sri Lankan government had implemented the Banda-Chelva Pact, this problem would not have happened! That's the main reason.

But that was not a separate state as such.

That was a federal state. A federal state means, they accepted the North and East as a Tamil homeland. But now we've lost that; we can [no longer] accept that sort of pact… We lost everything – our property and psychology, no? If they had honoured that pact, there would have been no problem. If they had honoured our parliamentary leaders and implemented their pact, the youth would never have taken up arms, and they would never have lost their lives. It's all for that reason.

Others blamed the political leaders:

• I think it's the politicians. Starting with Bandaranaike – he is the one who started the Sinhala Only policy. And then there was the standardisation policy.

So would you say it's mainly Sinhalese politicians?

I think so – yes, they are the ones who started it. And they are settling Sinhalese: for example, Batticaloa is a Tamil area, and they were settling Sinhalese in Batticaloa, Amparai and other Tamil areas. so that's also a problem. I think it's unfair to settle people like that.

So you think this is what led to the conflict?

Mainly, I think, it's the standardisation policy which is very unfair and ruined the country. If somebody has the better result, they should enter university, and that way you get better service for the country. They could have found a way to improve the economy rather than discriminating against the people who are coming up.

• Politics – cheap politics [is the cause]. In one word, that's the answer as far as I'm concerned: cheap politics.

You think it is politicians who have stirred up the trouble?

There's no question about it. I won't blame Sinhalese people. I have moved with them, and they are quite reasonable if they are left alone. But if you poison their minds, they can be easily twisted.

• It was all started by politicians for their own benefit and status – for their power and for their seats, they have developed that, formed that. They talk politics in parliament, there will be so many parties together around the table, they talk one thing there, in parliament, around their table; but they feed something else to the nation, they feed tension to the teenagers – this is what has happened.

Do you think the problem is caused only by Sinhalese politicians, or by both Sinhalese and Tamil politicians?

I strongly feel the Tamil politicians are also to blame. If they had been friendly in all matters, there is no chance that this situation would have developed. It is for their seats and power they have done all this. Definitely, a hundred times I will say, it hasn't been done by the community! We were good friends – there were so many intermarriages!

• I would say it's a man-made thing, made by the politicians. Sinhalese politicians have contributed more, and the Tamil politicians also have to be blamed. Anti-ethnic feeling is an easy way to run a political platform, to get an easy mandate; I think they have made the best use of it. The Sinhalese people's minds have been poisoned with anti-Tamil feeling, and almost all the Sinhalese have a feeling that Tamils have no homeland in Sri Lanka – which the Tamils have possessed… (Tamil politicians) have also used the same formula to attract the Tamil masses – using our ethnic feeling to get support.

This refugee, like many others, emphasised the distinction between Sinhalese political and religious leaders, and the Sinhalese people:

• The cause of the ethnic conflict is in the self-seeking politicians, so to say – politicians who are greedy for power and position, especially among the Sinhalese politicians. I think they are without exception very corrupt. Of course, the ordinary Sinhalese villagers lead simple lives and they are not bothered about whether you are a Tamil. But the politicians and the Buddhist clergy are ruthless.
Referring to the Buddhist clergy, last month, Mahanayake Thero – he is the chief priest of one of the sects – writes in one of the papers and says that this is a Sinhala Buddhist country and others must, in effect, obey – subordinate themselves – to the Sinhalese Buddhists. I can't understand at this stage – in these circumstances – how the responsible media should publish an article like that. These are things which incite people, so, in fact, I would also blame the media – the news media, including the television and radio.
So that is the thing; power-hungry politicians are the cause of the situation in Sri Lanka today. They don't for a moment look to the interests of the people as a whole, as human beings – you know, you may be Sinhalese, I may be Tamil or another man may be Muslim,

but then we're all human beings. They don't look at it from that point of view. Since 1958 or 1956 or since independence – we may as well say since Sri Lanka gained independence – the Sinhalese have taken over the administration of the country; from then onwards there has been discriminatory legislation, and then in 1983 they thought they could destroy the Tamils – it reached a climax in 1983.

What do they expect us to do? We can't all the time submit to their brutalities and atrocities and discriminatory methods. We had to defend ourselves against this, so naturally the boys showed them that we are not a servile race, and they started fighting. And now retribution has set in: now the Sinhalese are living in fear of their lives and Sinhalese people are being killed by their own people.

Discrimination, as these quotations show, was bitterly resented, and the resentment was not diminished by the constitutions of 1972 and 1978, which in effect defined Sri Lanka as a Sinhala-Buddhist country. But on top of that, it was the resurgence of anti-Tamil violence in the 1970s, and its rapid escalation after 1977 – especially the massive anti-Tamil riots in 1983 – which made more and more Tamils feel that the situation was intolerable, leading to the growth of a Tamil militant movement on the one hand, and the accelerated exodus of refugees on the other.

Discrimination against Tamils in university education and government employment would affect only a small minority, even if this was a relatively important section which would form the core of the militant movement; but the threat to their physical security was experienced by every Tamil, and led to the craving for some place where they could feel safe. In the initial stages, this place of refuge was not sought abroad by most Tamils, but in the Northern and Eastern Provinces where they could feel relatively secure – although in the Eastern Province the colonisation drives, leading to violence and attacks on Tamils, also contributed to Tamil insecurity.

The desire for a separate state, or at least for autonomy within a federal set-up, could never have gained popularity if it had not been seen as necessary for the attainment of basic rights and physical security:

> • The fact of the matter is, it is the refusal of successive Sinhala governments to concede the barest minimum concessions to the Tamils that has led to this imbroglio today.

Then you think this would not have happened if Tamil rights had been respected by the Sri Lankan government?

That's right. In 1947-8, what Chelvanayakam, the TULF leader, asked for was a federal set-up; they resorted to all manner of pleading – words, satyagraha, non-violent movements. This militancy has been something foreign to the Tamils in the recent past. Whenever they assaulted us, kicked us, we ran to Jaffna. We did not turn back to raise our hands. But if such passive people have been scored to a fever pitch of militancy, it is for this reason.

Some refugees saw violence as a prime cause of conflict:

• I was participating in the Fourth International Tamil Research Conference which was held in Jaffna during Mrs Bandaranaike's time, and 10 people were killed: that was the immediate cause for the uprising of Tamil youth. From that time, people started to raise arms and other things.

• A lot of people left Sri Lanka because of the Official Language Act; and in the hill country, it is so difficult to get into government employment because of the Act. Also, if you're stateless, you're not entitled to any employment in the public sector, and even the private sector won't take you. So very few people could get out of the plantation sector. Then there has been other legislation, and the two constitutions: the 1972 constitution which made Buddhism the state religion and gave the Sinhalese language itself a constitutional status, and the 1978 constitution by the UNP which made things worse – they didn't make things any better.
So there was all this discrimination, and along with it there was violence, from 1956 onwards. In the hill country, from 1970 particularly, estates have been burned, people have been killed – whenever there's been major violence, until recently it was not people in the North and East who suffered most, until the army was sent there; the Hill-country Tamils have been affected much more than anyone else. Discrimination, along with violence: this is what has caused the problem.

Others pointed to the links between discrimination and colonisation:

• The Tamil people have been denied their rights in every way by the Sri Lankan government. They feel they are a minority and can't live in Sri Lanka without getting their own country.

What exactly have they been denied?

Everything: getting jobs, getting education – and they have been settling Sinhalese people in the North and East, for example in the Vavuniya area, and Tamil people have been getting killed. Every time a Sinhalese party comes to power, they come to power through racist activities, through propaganda against Tamils.

• Sinhalese who are living in the Sinhala areas, I accept. But Sinhalese who have colonised and are living in the Tamil areas, I won't accept. Because they are not just Sinhala people – they are also one of the government institutions. They have taken our land.

What about the Sinhalese people who were living in Tamil areas before the government colonisation schemes?

In the East, before 1947 – you can get the census report – there were only 414 Sinhalese families in the Trincomalee district. But in 1987, there were three Sinhala areas in Trincomalee. In 1947, there were two Tamil areas in Trincomalee; in 1977, only one Tamil electorate.

The composition of the population has been shifted by these schemes?

Yes. They were forcibly brought there and colonised. They've brought people from prison, and other such anti-social elements. So in my view, they're not just ordinary Sinhalese people. Now also, I think, whoever comes to live with government support – prisoners or anti-social elements – they must realise that. Because in Sinhala areas they have a lot of land; so they can live and be prosperous. But they are coming to get our lands. If we lose our lands, we don't have a national identity… The way the British earlier treated all of us, Sinhalese and Tamils, after they left, the Sinhalese are treating us in the same way. That is the main reason why the problem started.

You think that is why the militants took up arms?

Yes. Till 1975, our political leaders fought by democratic means, through parliament, but they didn't achieve any of their aims. Finally, the Sinhalese government started to massacre Tamils – that was a very important turning-point. After that, there was no other way for Tamil youths to defend themselves and their people. That's the main reason why they took up arms. At that time, the government used to take people, put them in prison, kill them and throw their bodies in the road in the Northern and Eastern Provinces. Now it's happening in the South. So we are happy to see this happening in the South, because earlier the same thing happened in our areas, but at that time the Sinhalese were not worried about it. For them it is new, but for us this is old history.

So you think they took up arms basically to defend themselves?

Yes, basically to defend themselves and our people.

One described how students were provoked into violence:

• After 1971 the Sri Lanka Freedom Party, the SLFP, they imposed a law: standardisation. After that, most of the Tamil youths didn't get admission to university, so they were forced to lose their chances. To get their rights, they did some non-violent agitations; but the result was beatings and harassment. While they were unarmed, the state – the government, the police – answered with arms, so they were forced to take up arms.

Other refugees saw the land issue as fundamental to the conflict:

• They are settling Sinhalese by the hundred. The Sri Lankan government says, 'So long as you are a Ceylonese, you can settle anywhere.' That is not quite correct. I can go and buy in the South, and the Sinhalese can come and buy in the North. But here the *government* is settling the people. That is what we are against, not the Sinhalese ordinarily coming and residing. We are opposed to colonisation by the Sinhalese with government aid, not by people on their own: they can come and settle. That was the first thing, actually, the land. Then language, education, employment – there was discrimination.

Do you think that if it was not for the discrimination, there wouldn't have been a demand for a separate state?

Definitely not. Even if they had given a federal government, the demand would not have been there. Federalism, the politicians have been telling the Sinhalese since 1948, is separation. The media – the papers, the TV and the radio – have been saying that federalism is separation. So the Sinhalese masses are totally opposed to it, even now.

Even now, you think?

> Yes. It will be very difficult for the government to change their policy. Even if they agree to it, it will be very difficult to satisfy the Sinhalese masses. Because they have been told day in and day out, and brain-washed – you can say, brain-washed – that federalism is separation. Separation – we were forced to come to that position. Because when we asked for federalism they were killing us and putting us in jail and passing all sorts of legislation – even the MPs could not function in parliament because they were asked to take an oath that they would not advocate federalism. So they couldn't sit in parliament; there's so much discrimination!

Considering that these respondents spanned the entire political spectrum – from extreme Tamil nationalists, who supported and had participated in the armed struggle for a separate state, to vehement critics and opponents of Tamil nationalism – one central argument is remarkably consistent. Summed up, it would amount to something like this: successive Sinhalese governments and political leaders had alienated the Tamil-speaking minorities, and especially the youth, by a series of discriminatory measures in education and employment, by downgrading their language and culture, by Sinhalese colonisation of their areas, by denial of equal rights and equal opportunities, by anti-Tamil propaganda, and by the refusal of political autonomy. Repeated bouts of government-sponsored violence – either entirely gratuitous or in response to non-violent protests – had finally driven a section of Tamil youth to take up arms in self-defence and in order to establish a separate state of Tamil Eelam.

I was impressed by the fact that even the Tamil nationalists (including, incidentally, the one who had traced the ethnic conflict to pre-colonial times) did not claim that a separate Tamil state was somehow natural or historically inevitable, but, on the contrary, saw it as the solution to a very specific problem: namely, discrimination against and persecution of Tamils in Sri Lanka. I was also impressed by the refugees' inclination to pin-point specific policies rather than, say, more vaguely blaming Sinhalese people in general (an aspect which will be examined further in a later chapter).

The charge that government policies of discrimination and persecution have led to violent conflict has been confirmed by several non-Tamil observers, including one of the Sinhalese refugees. Indeed, it seems self-evident that measures aimed at progressively converting Sri Lanka into a Sinhala-Buddhist state must, necessarily, result in the denial of equal rights to ethnic minorities.

However, while this might be what initiated the process which has caused such massive displacement, it would be simplistic to see it as the sole cause of the present conflict; nor would it be possible to explain much of the displacement without referring to other factors. Many refugees referred to the opportunism of Tamil politicians and their willingness to play the ethnic and communal card; the activities of the Indian army (Peace-Keeping Force), which entered Sri Lanka after the signing of the Indo-Lanka Peace Accord in 1987, and of the militant group sponsored by them, the EPRLF (Eelam People's Revolutionary Liberation Front); the general progression of the Sri Lankan government towards totalitarian dictatorship; and competition for employment and in business.

Other factors were the more widespread poisoning of Sinhalese people's minds by anti-Tamil propaganda – resulting, among other things, in the JVP's opposition to any concession to Tamil demands; the rapid political degeneration of the Tamil movement, leading to murderous internecine fighting between the militant groups, out of which the LTTE emerged as the strongest; and the LTTE leadership's intolerance both of other groups and of opposition or criticism from Tamils, including their own membership.

Some refugees described how people, regardless of their allegiance, had been forced to live by the law of the gun:

> • They are sick of all this fighting. But now what has happened, in my opinion, is that the people who have got guns in their hands are not interested in finding out what the people want, they are only interested in what they themselves want. Anybody who disagrees with what they are thinking has to be killed. So many people have been killed [i.e. Tamils killed by Tamil militants]! The situation is that anybody who has a gun is important, and anybody who disagrees with this fellow with the gun is a target. It makes it all the more difficult for us to go back. If we go there, and while casually talking I say, 'I don't like that fellow', probably Tamils will shoot me. I mean, not that we are going to stand up on a platform and make a speech and then get shot – no! Just while talking, buying some vegetables in the market, if you casually mention something, probably that is good enough for being a target.

> • Everybody is with arms, anyone who has a gun has power, so it is difficult to say who is going to win or who is going to lose or how the situation is going to change. It is exactly like what's happening in Beirut.

• The government is not really prepared to do anything about the problem – they just go on and on with these talks and everything. And even the Tamil people – you know, the Tigers – they've got so used to the situation, I don't think they're aware of what's really going on. I mean, everyone's got used to the trend now: they fire, and these people attack. I don't know whether anybody gets a kick out of these things, but that's the way I see it: everyone's got used to this pattern of life, and they don't want to solve it – they just want it to be like that. And then the Indian army comes into it, and that's also enlarging the problem.

• In the last six months, it's been getting worse every day! Now, even small children are joining the boys' groups, because they are seeing people dying every day. They see innocent people getting killed, so they feel they don't want to live, at least they can catch one person and then they can die.

One problem for people was the number of factions involved:

• There are so many groups of Tamils, little, little groups; and in my opinion, I don't think there should be so many of those groups. If you're going to fight for freedom, you should be united. But this… I can't believe it! So many groups!

• I think it's the difference in their policies – like one group may have a policy, a couple of people don't like that, so they go and start a new group. I think this has added to the problems – like now, the IPKF are using the EPRLF against the Tigers. That's really a shame – I don't think it should be happening when we're fighting for our own freedom – we shouldn't have so many divisions among ourselves.

Some personal stories show that the struggle within the groups themselves had become destructive. For example:

• I worked in the LTTE, then I had a problem with the movement, so they sent me back to Jaffna. In Jaffna, I had trouble with them, so I left the movement.

Once you left, were you threatened? Death threats? Are there many people like you, who have left under threat?

Yes. They're hiding – at the moment, they're hiding. A lot of people.

So anyone who disagrees with the leadership very strongly has problems?

Yes. They must either leave the country or go into hiding – otherwise they'll be killed. There's no democracy now. Now we are also helping others who are hiding.

You mean former colleagues of yours from the movement who have also left?

Yes, yes. They've left, and they're in hiding. A lot of people – boys – are in that situation. Even today there were one or two letters from some of them in Colombo – they said, 'If you can send some money…' because they can't go to work in Colombo either – Colombo also is now full of all the movements, they are killing people…

Tamil movements operating in Colombo?

Yes! What has happened to Amirthalingam and Uma Maheshwaran and all these people? [Tamil leaders murdered by Tamil militants.] The government is supporting the LTTE – they give them houses and funds and that and this. So they are living and working there. And whoever comes from other movements, or their own former members, they get killed and dumped. Former members have the same problem as other movements: they can't live in Jaffna, they can't live in Colombo, they can't live in India… Not only that, even in Britain they are threatening us! We had decided to collect money through a programme and send it, and we printed tickets and sold the tickets. They threatened: 'Immediately you must stop this programme, otherwise you will lose one of your family members at home.' That's the main reason we stopped that programme.

They're threatening reprisals against your family members in Sri Lanka?

Yes, yes. Mainly the LTTE. So here also we are hiding – we can't do anything. They've been fighting each other, and they've lost their support from the people, so they've started doing all this.

The arrival of the Indian Peace-Keeping Force, according to several refugees, troubled the waters even further:

• Now the Indians have come, and they are discriminating between rival militant groups. They are trying to prop up a group [the EPRLF] which has no support with the people, and as a result they are killing everybody! They now say that they don't want to leave because the Tamils are not safe. It's all rubbish! The moment the IPKF leaves, I can assure you the EPRLF will be lynched by the people. They are waiting for an opportunity. Not because they love the Tigers, but because the EPRLF has committed so many atrocities. The conflict was started by the discrimination of the Sinhalese government; now it has been made worse by the discrimination of the IPKF.

• The Indians… like to look after their strategic interests, but they can't maintain the peace. They have no reason to kill our people: they came as a peace-keeping force! … I think the Indians must get out of our country, and they have to leave us to solve our problems in our own way. They are encouraging violence now. Yesterday I had a message from our village that the army had killed nearly about 200 people! They declared a curfew, and they said, 'We are searching for Tigers,' and they killed them. They said they came to keep the peace, but their behaviour shows that they have some other interest. It is true that we want peace, but there's no point talking about peace while the Indian army is killing people! They have to change their minds; they can stay here, but they have to change their minds.

• The Indian army came here as a peace-keeping force, but they're not doing their job properly. I think they are an 'Innocent People Killing Force'!

• We used to blame only the Sinhalese forces, but now we have to blame so many people: our own leaders, India… Those days we cried for help from India, we thought India will come and do something for our people, but the IPKF has not helped us! And at the moment, we don't have any unity among our people – we've got so many groups now… We believed in the Tigers and thought they would bring out something; but afterwards we became disillusioned, because they don't have real, proper people involved, with political knowledge and that sort of thing; they don't have enough knowledge.

• The main causes are political, economic, and now the Indian army there. Sinhalese jingoism asserts that foreigners invaded the country and controlled it. That's utter rubbish. It was always the ruling classes that invited the foreigners: Buvanekabahu invited the Portuguese, Rajasinghe II of Kandy invited the Dutch. And the miserable Kandyan chiefs, the ancestors of Mrs Sirimavo Bandaranaike, invited the British into Kandy. J.R. Jayawardene and clique invited the Indians into Sri Lanka – it's not the people of the country who invited them. They didn't come of their own accord.

What do you think actually started the trouble originally?

On both sides, the greed for political power by these leaders. Both sides, including Tamils: even now they're killing each other, it's only for power, not to serve the people. As has been said by one Tamil, 'It's like worm eating worm and growing fat.'

Some thought that to see the struggle as purely one between Tamils and Sinhalese was an over-simplification:

• Even among themselves they have a lot of differences, like, say Buddhist Sinhalese and Catholic Sinhalese, then up-country Sinhalese and low-country Sinhalese. Sinhalese discriminate among themselves and Tamils also discriminate among themselves – especially Jaffna Tamils. But when it comes to the fighting, it's Sinhalese and Tamils!

• Basically, the Sinhalese and Tamils are good people. I have been working and living with the Sinhalese – they are very hospitable people. But they have been charged with racism by the government, by successive governments, because that was the only weapon left to the government – I don't know how it was invented! – for them to come to power or to keep them in power.

Other interviewees were more philosophical:

• It's not only our leaders – it's also a lot of our people.

• The people also contributed, because the people also take responsibility for the mistakes if they follow bad leaders. There were lots of mistakes. It is not an unusual problem, because everywhere, in every country, you have a minority and a majority. There are so many countries with a majority and minority where they're living peacefully and prosperously, like Canada, Switzerland, even the United States. Even in India there is a majority and minority. But of course our political leaders, they made a contradiction out of this issue, they misused it, and they missed opportunities to solve the problem. Now they want to solve it, but the problem is complicated now – they are trapped by the complications, not by the problem itself…

• Actually, I'm optimistic. Because the problem must be solved. It is difficult, but we must find some sort of solution. In the past, nobody realised their mistakes, and they didn't want to realise them. Now I think everybody is beginning to realise them… I think with time they will agree on a common formula, a common solution. Because now everybody feels that we want a solution – it was not like that in the past. But the problem is so entrenched now, so complicated.

• Why are they killing innocent people? I don't know why Sinhala people or Tamil people are killing innocent people… Fighting between militant groups and government troops is one thing, but killing innocent people is very, very bad. Every person, from whatever party, has rights. They have the right to support any party without getting killed for it. I don't know what's the meaning of this kind of 'revolution'! They're just after power, I think.

We will return to the question of the relationship between the communities at a later stage, when considering solutions to the problem; for the moment, what is important is that so few respondents thought that ethnic differences in themselves were a cause of the conflict, although some did point out that constant anti-Tamil propaganda had poisoned the minds of many Sinhalese.

We have been through a diversity of views on the causes of the conflict, and if the picture that emerges is complicated – even confusing – this is to a large extent due to the nature of the reality itself. Unless the complexity of that reality is grasped, it will be impossible to understand the different reasons why refugees have been fleeing the country.

Chapter 2: Flight

When the refugee problem first began to take on serious proportions after the 1983 riots, there was a more or less uniform cause of flight: government-sponsored violence in the form of pogroms, reprisals against civilians, and torture and extra-judicial executions facilitated by the Prevention of Terrorism Act (PTA) 1979. This Act provided for a person to be detained incommunicado for up to 18 months without being charged or brought before a magistrate, and had no provision for legal remedies for detention or torture.

By mid-1989, the situation had become far more complicated; the refugees might be fleeing the Sri Lankan security forces, the Indian army, the EPRLF, the Tigers, some combination of these forces, or the crossfire between them, in a 'dirty' war in which all sides engaged in atrocities against civilians, including little children.

We turn now to the experiences which led to their decision to leave – or, in some cases, to their relatives' decision to make them leave. The accounts which follow are all compatible with reports published by Amnesty International and other human rights organisations, as well as published accounts by Sri Lankan writers and analysts; there seems to be no reason for doubting their authenticity. Yet only those marked with an 'R' at the end of their statements had been given refugee status; none had received political asylum.

> • I was working in Air Lanka. In 1985, Tamil militants bombed the Tristar, and after that they were suspicious about us, Tamils working there. And they caught two of my colleagues, two Tamils – caught them and took them to the CID.

Were they involved in the bombing?

> They were not involved, but they were suspected. One came on holiday to the UK, I think, on the day of that particular incident. The other one, I don't know why they suspected him. They were taken to the CID, fourth floor [notorious for the torture carried out there] and interrogated.

Tortured?

> Yes. They are still there. The CID had gone to one Tamil engineer's house and questioned him at 2 o'clock in the night, and they asked him what's my address, to go to my place, and fortunately he didn't

know my address and didn't lead them to me. Then one day while I was working, the call came to me stating that the CID wants to speak to me. I went there – I hadn't been involved in anything.

They started questioning me: 'Why are you going to London at times, who do you know there, are you supporting these militants, where do you get money, who gives you money for going abroad?' We get free tickets because we work for the airline, but still they were asking me all these things. My family was not staying with me – they were in Jaffna, my daughter and my wife – so I was worried about them too. Because one of my brothers-in-law had been shot in Vavuniya in 1983: on the way to Jaffna, they kidnapped the bus and shot about 18 Tamils. One of them was my only sister's husband.

Do you know who did that?

The army. Because there was an attack on the army camp by the Tamil militants, and this was in retaliation for that. So ultimately I also got panicky, I was afraid to stay there, so I took my leave and came over here with my wife and daughter.

• In 1984 I was arrested by the Sri Lankan army, beaten with a gun barrel and kicked. My mother was able to speak in Sinhala, so she managed to get me released.

What was the reason — did they give you any reason?

At that time one inspector was shot dead, so they rounded up the area and took some youths and harassed them.

• In 1981 I started working in Saudi Arabia, and my family was occupying a flat in Colombo. In the 1983 riots the house was attacked and ransacked; my family had to leave the house and stay temporarily with Sinhalese neighbours, then go to the refugee camp, and then they were shipped to Jaffna. But I thought, even in Jaffna it was not safe – the army, the Sinhalese army, was moving around and shooting and killing. So I decided to remove them all out of Sri Lanka, and later I joined them.

• I was one of those who suffered in the July 1983 riots. In Badulla, where my house was burned, we ended up as refugees in a refugee camp – my wife and I. And then we were sent to Jaffna. I had been in Badulla for 32 years, practising as a lawyer there, when the situation became very unsettled and critical – in Jaffna also, because of the clashes between the Sri Lankan army, the police and the Tamil militants. The police station in my home town was destroyed by the militants, and also the courts. Then, because my children were rather concerned about our lives, they persuaded my wife and me to come out to London.

• I decided to leave Sri Lanka mainly because of my children's future – I have one daughter aged 20, and after 14 years I had a son – he's only 6. We had problems with these groups – they come to our school and demand one day's salary and all that. And they come home asking for food parcels… The Tigers were asking for money and jewellery. But later, under the IPKF, the EPRLF started stealing everywhere. There were cases of rape, even of married women. But before the IPKF came, there was such a lot of shelling, we couldn't get out for even half an hour because we didn't know when the helicopter would come; you just had to run about, get some bread and all that, and come back. Many times I have got caught at it – people start shooting from the helicopters, and we just run into any house we know on the way. One of our school children also died like that – a seven-year-old – a shell fell right on his head. Amazing to think of all that now: my son might have been another victim if he had stayed longer.

• I worked for the Sri Lankan government for 14 years as a trustworthy employee; they wanted me to study Sinhala so I studied Sinhala, I passed their language at SSC level, I worked for them without any disagreement or misunderstanding. But unfortunately my brother – one of my younger brothers – got involved in the movement; he was detained, he escaped from prison, and he was wanted by the government. I saw him after about seven years in 1985 – he came to know where I was and he came to my place. At that time we were staying in government quarters, and he came to see me there one day. The purpose he came for was to get some assistance for the refugees, people who were fleeing from other places to Vavuniya. At that time I didn't want to see him because I wanted to avoid any political involvement – it was a very sensitive area, on the Sinhalese and Tamil border, and we were living close to the army and police station… But he was my brother, you know, I couldn't say no, so I gave him some money. He came a second time also, with another two boys. I think somebody saw him and gave the message to the army or police that some of the boys are coming to my place, so they thought I was fully involved in the movement. Luckily, I knew someone in the police department; he telephoned me and said, 'There is a charge against you under the Prevention of Terrorism Act – they are going to arrest you for sure. If it's possible, try to get away from your place.' That day the army surrounded my house – there were 34 armed guards! But I was not there. The next day my wife came to Jaffna and said, 'You must get out of this country somehow.' So within five days I left.

• Well, the story is like this. In 1983 my house near Colombo was burnt. Five of them came to the house, you see. I was the only man. My second son and my wife managed to hide; my elder son and I got the beating. I got two bones broken and all that. So I shifted to Batticaloa because we have some property there. Then I found that my younger son was very much affected by what happened.

He saw what happened?

Of course! They were hiding and seeing what was happening. He was 8 or 9 when that happened. After that, his teacher used to tell me, 'Your son is fairly badly affected. If I ask him to write about a dog, he will say, 'The dog was barking when my house was burned.' If I ask him to write about the moon, 'The moon was shining when my house was burned.' To write about a tree, he will say, 'The people who burned my house cut down the tree that was in front of it.' You know, whatever he was asked, this was having an effect on it. He kept telling me, 'Papa, you could have easily fought those fellows, and you could have easily hit them, but you never made an attempt'. Then the teacher told me, when they asked the students, 'What is your ambition in life?' my son had said, 'When I grow up, I'll become a Tiger and shoot at least a hundred Sinhalese.' That shocked me. I didn't want that to happen. I thought that if I went to India, I would lose my son [because the Tamil militant groups were active in India too], so I wanted to go somewhere else.

My house was attacked for a second time, in Batticaloa, in April 1985. So it was just a matter of days when we decided to leave. People were getting shot dead for nothing. I was seeing corpses all over the place.

• You know in Amparai, all communities are living together – Muslims, Tamils and Sinhalese. In one of the incidents in 1985, my younger brother was killed by the STF – in May 1985. [The Special

Task Force was a paramilitary unit whose numerous atrocities against both Tamils and Sinhalese have been well documented.]

Was he involved in any of the groups?

No. On Friday morning, the STF came. The reason is that the day before, the Tamil militants had killed some Sinhalese in Anuradhapura. The day after that, this incident happened. They came and fired at random. Then in 1986 May, at Rambukkana, when I travelled from Kandy to Colombo, some Sinhalese said I'm a Kotiya [Tiger]. They had gone to the station-master, I think; he asked me to get down from the train and took me to the police, and they arrested me.

How long were you in detention?

Three days.

Were you ill-treated?

Yes.

So were these the main reasons why you left?

There were some others too. I couldn't go to my village because of the STF – any time they can come and arrest or shoot. So when I finished my degree I went to Kandy, then I went to Colombo, stayed there and found a teaching job. But in the holidays I went to my village, and I had some problems with the militant groups there as well. Some things were going wrong… But when you try to explain, when you try to criticise them, then you will be on the list. I face that sort of problem. On all sides I faced problems. [Then I received] a death-threat from the militant groups – that was the most important reason why I left. I left the following day.

• In the army operations in the northern part of Sri Lanka, so many young people have been arrested, including me at one time – in 1986. After that I could not go to college, so my parents said I should go to another country rather than live there, because I may be arrested. My friends also have been arrested and disappeared.

This is by the security forces, is it?

Yes.

• Since leaving school, after the riots in 1956, I was engaged in farm development work and public development work and social work in the Northern Province, and I used to address public meetings also. But then the boys started fighting, they went into the jungle and started their training, and the police started to suspect me because they thought I was encouraging them in various ways. So they arrested me. That was in 1979.

I was put in a cell for a week. They didn't look after me properly, and they wanted me to make a statement saying that I had been participating in activities which I had not actually participated in. I refused, and some of the other social workers met the police officers and said that I was not involved in these things, so they released me. But they went to my home and they took all these files and papers, and they found that some of the books were written by Chelvanayakam, so again they started suspecting me because I was having those documents. This finally made it difficult to stay in that country – I thought that it's not safe for me to remain there, and I decided to leave the country.

• The shelling… you don't know when it will fall and where it will fall. It has fallen around my house – that area – but you really don't know when it will fall on your house. And sometimes they ask you to get out of the house and stay in the temple or somewhere for six days, saying that they are going to check the house and all that. So… I used to be so scared, because the army means you are so scared…

This was the Sri Lankan army?

The Sri Lankan army – it's a Sinhalese army! I mean the thing is, you can't live there – it's impossible. You can't live there because of the trouble, the shooting and all that.

• I had been involved in political activities since 1980. I was working for the LTTE as a full-timer in 1983, so I was a 'noted' [officially recorded] case. The Sri Lankan army would come to my place to check whether I was there, because I was involved in military activities. I was arrested in 1984, tortured and detained for one week – the army wanted to find out where the Tiger camp was and where they were living, so they were rounding up all the young boys from Jaffna town and torturing them to get this information.

After that incident I decided to leave the country because when I'd been caught I gave a different name, and that was the only way I was able to escape from detention. I realised that if I stayed there, I would get caught and tortured again. So I thought it would be better to leave the country. I was able to get a passport immediately by giving some money to an agency, and I left in January 1985 with a visa to East Germany.

• I was kicked out of Sri Lanka. I was put on a flight to Britain, that's all. I was given two days' notice, and my brother told me that he'd bought my ticket for me and I should go. I had done my 'O' Levels and I wanted to do my 'A' Levels as usual, and I was doing my 'A' Levels at that time when the 1983 riots came up. And before the 1983 riots I was also involved in certain other things that my brother didn't like – that my family didn't like: I joined the EROS and everything else. So when the crunch came, they already had got in touch with the college in England; they managed to get my admission, and told me victoriously before my departure. I mean, had they told me earlier, I wouldn't have left anywhere.

So it was your family who got you to leave?

Yes – they are the people who trapped me here. I think it's because one of my classmates got arrested. His uncle and my family are good friends, and he probably informed them.

• When I was in Sri Lanka I was participating in anti-government activities, and I mostly joined with the TULF [the Tamil parliamentary party]. From that day I was 'noted'. In 1972 I organised a demonstration, hartal [general work stoppage], and everything. One day the military personnel came to my house and tried to arrest me, I escaped with gun-shot wounds. Three or four days later I came here, with 25 stitches in my leg. I had treatment in a hospital.

So you left immediately?

Yes, that was the last day I spent in my house – I never went back. From there I went to a safe place, until I could come to Colombo. Before that, when I returned from India, I had been arrested and kept for 15 days in detention. That was in 1981. They tortured me – my diaphragm was broken, so I had to go to hospital. Jaffna hospital. For ten days they kept me in the camp near the bus stand at Vavuniya; then they took me to the police station. From there I contacted my uncle, and only after that was I released.

It was terrible! They hang you upside down and they light a fire in a pot and put chili powder on it – they did that, that time. They beat me on the back, pulled out nails from my feet – terrible torture! In those 10 days I suffered a lot. They broke my nose, and they punched me in the stomach…

• The Sri Lankan army was shelling, and bombing from helicopters, and so many things – even near to my house, so many people got killed, because they were shelling without looking here or there, they were just shelling. One day when I went near the town I had a narrow escape, because a bomber was bombing and so many people got killed. So my mind was very upset, I had no peace of mind. My father, my mother, everybody wanted me to go away, to leave the country, otherwise maybe I could get killed. So they asked me to leave as soon as possible.

• We were living in Colombo, and our house was burned in 1983. Then we went to Batticaloa, which is our home town, where we lived for about a year and a half. What really made us decide to come here was that there was some sort of problem between the Muslims and Tamils, I think. The Muslims [she is referring to the Muslim Home Guards, a government paramilitary unit] started burning houses and villages one after the other – they almost came to our village, so that night no one slept. The whole village was up, and we were wondering whether we were going to get killed by the army.

They killed and they burned systematically, village by village. First they burned one village and all the houses in that village, then they went on to the next village. This was done by the Muslims [Home Guards] and the army, together – the army was protecting the Muslims [Home Guards] while they were burning the houses.

My husband was in Colombo, only my son and I were in Batticaloa. We actually went to the lagoon and we were hiding behind the shrubs and the bushes. Because the army came in an armoured car, and they had some powerful light, so the people couldn't even hide. We were so scared! That whole night we stayed out – on the bank of the lagoon we were hiding. It was a terrible night! And we could see the fires – we could see the other villages being burned, because the thing was such that the villages were alongside the lagoon, and if you stand in one part of the lagoon, you could see the rest of the villages, so we could see the houses being burned and people screaming and shouting. It was a terrifying night; we didn't think we would survive that night.

Luckily for us, just before they came to our village – two villages before they came to our village – at that point it was 4 o'clock in the morning, and Muslims, they have to go to pray. So because they had to go to the mosque to pray, they stopped, and we were saved.

We were so frightened on that night, my son was also crying. I said, 'Don't get scared, we'll all die together.' But he says, 'I don't want to die, I want to live, I don't want to die!' That night I telephoned my husband, and in about two or three days we left. Partly it was because we had no home; because we came from Colombo to Batticaloa thinking that we would be safe, but then we thought that next time we would have to jump into the sea!

• My twin brother was in one of the movements, so I was afraid they would identify me with him. He died on 19th March, this year – killed by the IPKF.

Did you manage to get a proper passport and visa to come to Britain?

No. I got a forged Sri Lankan passport, but not in my name. An agent got me a visa.

• I passed out as an advocate for the Supreme Court of Sri Lanka, and for some time I was practising as Crown Counsel. Thereafter I joined the Legal Draughtsmen's department. But I was denied promotional chances, and whenever scholarships were offered, I was overlooked. So I petitioned against my seniors, saying that things were going badly and all that. From that time onwards, the higher-ups as well as my Sinhalese colleagues developed some kind of hatred towards me. I was asking for my rights, but they interpreted it otherwise.

You felt you were being discriminated against?

Not felt; in fact I was. You see, I was the seniormost among the Tamils in that department, and should have been made a Deputy Legal Draughtsman long, long ago. But they would always say, 'Yes, because the Deputy Legal Draughtsman's post involves a lot of administrative work… Of course you have passed your GCE exam in Sinhala, but that is not sufficient.' And they always used that as an excuse to shut me out. Then an opportunity came from Nigeria – the government of Sokoto recruited me as a lecturer in law in one of the polytechnics – and it was a big amount that was offered, so I thought that rather than be discriminated against in Sri Lanka, I would go.

Was it because you came to the end of your contract that you came to Britain?

The end of the contract, yes. I can't think of going back just now, because things have worsened – I would not be safe in the hands of the Sri Lankan forces, or the Indian forces, or in the hands of the militants sponsored by them, I don't think.

• I was involved in refugee resettlement in the Vavuniya area, and I was working with EROS at that time, and also with TRRO – Tamil Refugee Rehabilitation Organisation. They were Hill-country Tamils who had been driven out of the plantations. We were educating them and finding almost all the resources for resettling them in those areas. This was in 1977. By 1979, they were raiding almost all the organisations; they arrested eleven of our people from the Vavuniya area, and they were looking for me. So they came to the college where I was teaching, then to my house, and they took my uncle, then went to the next house and took my cousin. My uncle was imprisoned, and they were taking too many people instead of me, because they didn't know what I look like, so they took another person instead of me, an engineer's wife – and they were actually giving trouble to some other ladies as well.

Was this the security forces?

Yes, the Sri Lankan army. So I thought that if they came to know that I've left the country, then they might leave my uncle and they won't give trouble to the other people as well. So I had to come out – I was forced to leave my country and go to India.

What made you leave India and come to Britain?

In India I was actually involved in a political campaign, and was also organising rehabilitation work for the estate workers who had been deported under the Sirimavo-Shastri Pact [see Chronology]. Eventually the Indian government asked me to leave the country.

• The first time we left Colombo was after the racial riots in 1983. Our house was attacked, so we had to run to the refugee camp in Kotahena, then from there we had to go to the harbour, and then to the Northern Province by the ship provided by the Indian government. We were in Velvettiturai for some time, and we put our children into schools there. But again those schools were bombed from the sea by the navy and my house was burned. To safeguard our lives, we had to go back to Colombo. In the meantime I got this scholarship, so I had to go to Australia to follow it. But my family suffered a lot – they were going from Colombo to Velvettiturai and back, the children couldn't get any continuous education – everything was disturbed. So they came to Britain, and I joined them from Australia.

• There was some real danger for my life at my workplace, and also at my residence. Because I used to work in the Sri Lankan army – not as a soldier, but in the administration. Then I took up accountancy, and was appointed at the IGP's office – that is police headquarters. Most of the top-ranking army and police officers were personally known to me, and they knew me also, and they were the people operating in Vavuniya. My duties involved liaising with them. And the activities of the police and the government machinery then, were in search of the so-called militants. So my duty also was supposed to be to trace the militants and hand them over the military! That was very unfortunate.

The place where I was working was the birthplace of all the Tamil groups. Our part of the duty, officially, was to spot them out, where they were, and inform the police and the army, so that the police and the army could come and arrest them and do whatever they like. It was not a pleasant job. Being a state officer, I had to do certain things; but I never did this thing of informing on these people. I had a problem with the militants also, because I never acted in any way against my own conscience. But the army distrusted me, because they expected me to give them more assistance, but it was not forthcoming,

So ultimately, when they came to know that it was not forthcoming, they really turned against me. One day they came to my office and shot 50 rounds, and one night they came for me in four or five army trucks. I was alone there, my family was in Jaffna at the time, so I quietly slipped away through the back entrance of the quarters. But just near my gate, there was a statue of Arumuga Navalar, the great Hindu saint; they broke that statue of Navalar into pieces, urinated on it, and also damaged my gate.

Then you know there was Gandhiyam [rehabilitation scheme], Dr Balasunderam was carrying on a lot of work there for rehabilitating refugees – he was not involved to my knowledge in any activity other than rehabilitating some upcountry Tamils who had been uprooted. But the government intention was not to help them!

You must have heard of the Dollar and Kent Farms? Originally they were for the rehabilitation and settlement of these uprooted Tamils. The farms were not really on encroached state land; they were farms given to certain companies, like the Dollar Corporation. Big business concerns were given land, up to some 600 acres, under the Dudley Senanayake government. So when they abandoned that land because of Sinhala colonisation and harassment and that sort of thing, they allowed the land to be settled by people who had lost their homes in the upcountry. But when that was taking place, the government was not really happy: they wanted them to be chased out. [They did eventually succeed in chasing out these hapless people, making them refugees once more, and resettled the farms with Sinhalese convicts and their families.]

But they encouraged Sinhalese people to encroach on state lands! Adjacent areas were being encroached on by Sinhalese people, without any permit. And there were bhikkus [Buddhist monks] coming and settling in the areas of tanks [reservoirs], bringing some Sinhalese people. They would get hold of the district minister, get the tank renovated, make it a permanent settlement – and not only that, they also renamed the places! So we couldn't actually work according to our conscience.

That was the situation then: we were at the centre of all these activities – Gandhiyam, Sinhala colonisation, training of these boys and everything. We, as state officers, were supposed to be with the government – to prevent Tamils encroaching on state lands, to assist the army to chase out the Tamils and bring the Sinhalese into these areas – but I couldn't comply with them. I had some good Sinhalese friends who were very close to the army officers, and one of them one day told me, 'It's not safe for you to stay here, better get out from the place, don't sleep at your quarters, they are after you,' So the message was clear for me, and I thought it was time to leave; even the government agent told me it was better to leave, because I was more marked than any of the other people there.

But at that time, we believed there was going to be some settlement or intervention on the Indian side, and if there was any settlement between the Sinhalese and Tamil people, that was the only thing we wanted. That is the real reason I didn't come as a refugee. I applied for six months' leave and came, thinking that after six months I could go back; but I found that I couldn't.

• I left because of the problems that were happening around me – say people were arrested, people being charged – things like that. I went with a few of my colleagues on a human rights survey to Batticaloa after the riots, and we were taken for questioning while we were doing the survey. We were quite 'noted' then, but because we were lawyers we were able to escape without too much harassment. In those days when you said you were a lawyer, they were willing to listen. After that, my friend and I thought we would be out for some time, and then another friend was thinking about opening a Tamil Information Centre. So we left.

• I was in the eighth grade, and I was actually in school when my grandmother came and got me at mid-day because all the troubles were breaking out on the street; and that's how it started. This was July 1983 – in Colombo. Then we went to Jaffna, where there wasn't any trouble at that time. We had Indian ships coming to take us there, and I studied there for one year, finishing my eighth grade.

Then I started my ninth grade, but then the army started bombing from the sea, and we had to go to our granddad's house through all these lanes and jumping over the fence and everything, because the main forces of the army were coming. So we – all the family – went to Colombo again, because by this time it was Jaffna which was getting into trouble. Then I went to one of the other schools again and tried to finish the ninth grade, and then back to another school. That was in 1985, and that's when we came to Britain. It was very sudden. We'd got a school holiday, and I remember just owing some money to one of my friends because everything was so sudden.

• In 1983 we were very much disturbed by the riots in Colombo – we lost our jewellery, property, everything. Then we went to Velvettiturai, but after six months there was a problem there also. My children were studying there, but then their school was burned. I tried to contact my husband because he was living in Colombo, working there, but I couldn't contact him – there were no phones, nothing. Every day there were problems, no schools, and the army bombed, all the time they bombed.

That was in 1984. I went back to Colombo to join my husband, but then he got a scholarship and went to Australia. I couldn't live alone with my children in Velvettiturai. Every day they were coming, the army people were coming in a jeep and killing people. They were catching 17-year-old boys. At that time, my son was 16 or something, I was frightened that he would get caught. So we decided to come to Britain, because my brothers are here. Only for one year, we thought; after that, everything will be sorted out, we thought. But after that, the problem was worse. We thought we couldn't go back.

• I was doing some serious study because I really wanted to enter the university, but you couldn't continue peacefully – all the time there was something going on, and the situation was getting worse and worse and worse. Then the Tigers and others were coming and pushing us to join them and all that. They just came into the school. Our principal was really strict – she wouldn't allow us to go and join – so later on they'd get admission at gun-point, so she couldn't do anything. They just come in and have a meeting, and say 'Sign this form' and all that. Some of the girls joined, and a couple of them died in the fight, I heard later on.

Did you join?

No, I never did. I was really scared, for a start; and also I didn't know which group to support, there were so many of them!

Was that one of the reasons why you decided to leave?

Yes – my parents took that really seriously, you know, they were scared for me and my brother. He's really small now, but when he grows up, he may go automatically into that sort of thing.

• I left because of the political problems. In '86 when I was there in Jaffna, near my house there was the Tiger movement, so the Sri Lankan army started bombing… We couldn't stay there because the children were screaming, every day and night we couldn't sleep, we were thinking, 'What is going to happen the next day?' My husband was not there at the time – he was in Colombo, working there.

I wrote a letter to my sister in Britain, she wrote a sponsor letter to me, and I got a visa for three months. So I came with my children, and straightaway I asked for political asylum, at the airport. My husband stayed in Colombo, and I felt very sorry about that, because the children are very small, and I got a letter from my relations that he was arrested in Wellawatte, Colombo, because they thought he was involved with the political movements. I was very unhappy and depressed. After that, this year, he came and joined me; but he couldn't come straight away, he came illegally, because this government wouldn't allow him to come and join me.

How long was he in detention?

Two months. In Wellawatte prison. Then he went to Jaffna, but he had difficulty in getting food and staying at home because the IPKF asked him to come to the camp. Now he is with me and my children. We still don't know about our stay – but at least we are safe in this country.

• The army assaulted me because I was a member of a militant group. I was detained for 35 days, then again for three months. Then, after the arrival of the IPKF, they used to take me daily and bring me back.

Who used to take you?

First the Sri Lankan army, then the IPKF – to prevent us from going back to the movement, to have us under control, they took us daily.

Were you tortured when you were in detention?

Yes. [Shows injuries on throat and chest.] I had been assaulted to such an extent and injured so badly that I wanted to get medical treatment, I wanted to get out of the country and get myself treated – that was the main reason I decided to leave. They beat me with a PVC pipe, attacked various parts of my body including the genitals, burned me with cigarettes, caused a lot of injuries. I am still in a deteriorated condition. Within a year I have to undergo an operation on the hips, otherwise in another few years' time I may not be able to get up and walk about.

• You know, in Sri Lanka, basic human rights have been violated; people are unable to talk freely, they are unable to write, and their day-to-day life is endangered. Physically we are at risk, our lives are at risk from a lot of directions – from the Sri Lankan troops, the Indian troops, and from the division and unplanned struggle among the militant groups. All of them pose a risk to our lives. My house has been burgled and partly destroyed by Indian troops and by the militant Tamil groups and by the Sri Lankan troops. So I had a very empty feeling – I couldn't breathe the air of freedom. I was so depressed, I thought of leaving.

• I was in Jaffna when the war erupted between the LTTE and the IPKF. When the IPKF captured our hospital, you know that they killed many people inside the hospital. The war erupted on the 10th of October, and they came to our hospital on the 21st and 22nd of October. One of my consultants and one of my colleagues were killed. So after two months I came down to Colombo. Then my brother, who is in Switzerland, contacted me and said, 'You can make a visit to Switzerland.' So I went to Switzerland, and then came to Britain.

• We left because we underwent persecution; UNP thugs came to attack our house and they came to kill us. At that time the UNP was in power, during the 1983 riots. They took over that place, took over Nawalapitiya. The UNP people were like most thugs, they were not an educated crowd, all uneducated people were there. And we were the only Jaffna Tamils there at the time. When these thugs were coming, when they were burning the town, the Sinhalese man in the upper house – actually he belongs to that JVP crowd – he was a really nice chap, he came running from the hospital and he said, 'The mob is coming, come, close the house and come.' And he took us to his house. We were watching when they came and damaged the house – about 50 people. From the upper house we were watching them searching down below – they were searching for us… Then they left the house and went off. My children were small at the time, and they were very scared. One son asked me whether we should kill ourselves before they come and shoot us. When they said that to me, I felt very bad; I felt it was my duty to get them to a better place.

For two days we were staying with this boy, then some Sinhalese neighbours came and scared him; they said, 'If you keep them, you'll also get into trouble, so send them to the camp.' So we went to the refugee camp and stayed for two days, but then that boy felt sorry, and he came and called us back to his house, and we were there with him for ten days. Then we hired a van and went to Jaffna – we left everything like that and went to Jaffna.

At that point we thought, what's the purpose in staying? Because that house actually belongs to my husband, his parents were there for a very long time, the house was there for nearly 30-40 years... If you are not recognised in your own country, in your own birthplace, then what's the purpose of staying there?

• I was arrested by the Sri Lankan army in January 1984, and was in detention for nearly two years, until November 1985. They arrested me in my home, then they took me to Maskeliya in the central part of Sri Lanka, near Nuwara Eliya. I have been in the Vavuniya army camp, Maskeliya, Hatton, Welikada, Tangalle, Boosa... My mother came to visit me after nearly 19 or 20 months, with great difficulty – and she had to find money.

Do you know why you were arrested?

I was involved in politics in one of the groups, and I am interested in estate Tamils [Hill-country Tamils], so I took classes for them – not politics classes, just ordinary classes – in Hatton College, on Saturdays and Sundays, when I was at Peradeniya [university]. So the Maskeliya police arrested me, because I had been in Maskeliya with some boys. They came to Vavuniya army camp, and took some army people, and came to my house and surrounded it. I couldn't escape... Somebody arrested before me had mentioned my name under torture. I went through all kinds of torture – they put pins in my nails, they hung me upside down and beat me, they did so many things – I have even written a leaflet about what happened to me in Sri Lankan prisons.

Then my mother gave 80,000 rupees to get me released. I was arrested under the Sri Lankan Prevention of Terrorism Act; according to that Act, after 18 months they must bring me to court. But they didn't – they wanted to keep me. So afterwards my mother gave the money – she gave nearly 50,000, and she spent another 30,000. So they spent nearly 80,000 rupees to get me released.

Was that when you decided to try and leave Sri Lanka?

Yes. After that, twice the army came to my house to arrest me. But I was not there, I was in hiding... I paid money to an agent to get my travel documents. He got me a passport, but not a visa – I came without a visa. I came through India – I was there for 10 days. At the airport in Britain they gave me temporary admission, and I claimed political asylum. After two or three months, they asked me to go back to India: they said that I came through India, so I could ask for asylum in India also. But I don't want to go there, because I was a member of a political group – a militant group – so it's difficult for me there. Then I got a stay order because they wanted to deport me. They treat me as an economic refugee – even though I've got all the documents, I've got the detention order!

So they didn't believe you?

They didn't believe me. They said the reason was that I could have asked for asylum in India, so why did I choose a European country?

• In 1987, every day the Sri Lankan army was bombing and carrying out air attacks. I couldn't live there; all the time there was bombing and shelling – I can't live like that. I also had a problem with the Tigers. I support the other movement – not the Tigers – so they made some trouble for me, the Tigers. I couldn't stay there with the Sri Lankan army problem and the Tiger problem.

• One of my brothers was arrested in June 1986 and killed. My second brother was also beaten by the army one time… and he had to go to hospital for nearly three months. I'm the third brother, so they decided to send me. My father's a sick person, someone has to help – that's why my elder brother stayed behind; but he said, 'You leave the country and save your life.' At first I didn't want to go, because my parents really helped me, and I wanted to stay with them – I really like my parents. But my parents and my brother said, 'You must go, otherwise we won't let you stay in our home, go away now!' – something like that. They asked an agency to get me a passport and visa, but the agency cheated us – it was a forged visa.

• I am the youngest in the family – I've got two sisters, father and mother in Sri Lanka. Some of my friends are in the movements, they are fully involved. That means, if they are caught by the Sri Lankan army, they would give my name also, and the Sri Lankan army would find out about me – that was one problem. Another problem is in the movement itself. One is the Tigers, but I supported the other movement, so they tried to kill us… My father didn't like me to stay there because I was young; he said, 'You must leave – just go to any part of the world you want to go to.' That was another reason…

I decided to leave very suddenly. In 1986 July I was still at college, but I couldn't continue studying because two or three times I was involved with the Sri Lankan army. One time they killed one of my friends – both of us were coming on bicycles, and suddenly they were in front of us, the Ceylon forces, and they shot and killed my friend. I just left my bicycle and ran away, far away. Then I came back after two hours' time, he was still lying there. I didn't want to stay after that… My father paid an agent to get my travel documents.

• I decided to leave Sri Lanka because my children's studies were being disrupted. Another problem was that my husband was in the government, no? So one of the boys, the LTTE movement boys, said, 'Your husband helped the Sri Lankan government.' The army said, 'Your husband helped the boys.' So we had a problem with both parties. I have two sons; the elder one is grown up, and the movement wanted him to join, they asked him to join. They ask for money and everything – I have given some money, yes…

I had already decided to come to Britain, because of this two-sided problem. My husband had come with only a six-month visa. I left my children in Jaffna in the care of my father-in-law and went to the British High Commission in Colombo and said that I want to join my husband in Britain, I have a problem looking after my two sons alone, and I asked for a visa. I waited three months. First the High Commission said, 'You wait for one month.' I waited for one month by myself – the children were in Jaffna, and there was a lot of fighting there between the Sri Lankan government and the boys. People were saying my children's school was bombed – I was anxious and fed up, for one month I was suffering in Colombo! After a month they didn't reply, so I went back to Jaffna. Then a friend took up my case with the British High Commissioner in Colombo, and the Home Office, but still they never replied.

So after three months, you and your children came without a visa?

Yes, without a visa.

• I was actually involved in one of the movements. Then I left the movement, so they passed the order to kill me. So they were searching for me on one side, and the Sinhala army was searching on the other side – I was trapped. There was no one to help me in my situation. So that's the reason I left, because actually I was involved in the LTTE movement, the Tigers.

So when did you decide to leave Sri Lanka?

When I left the movement. I couldn't get a passport, because if I wanted to get a passport, I'd have to go to Colombo, and they would have arrested me – I couldn't get through the barrier at Elephant Pass [the narrow pass connecting the Jaffna peninsula to the rest of Sri Lanka]. So actually, anyone who was involved in the movements or participated in the political struggle couldn't go to Colombo and get proper documents. So an easy way was to cross the Palk Strait by boat and go to Madras, and the agencies would arrange for travel to Bombay, and from Bombay abroad.

I contacted an agent, and he arranged everything. There are a lot of agencies operating there – if you pay the money, they arrange everything, false documents and ticket. I wanted to go to Canada, and bought a ticket with London as a transit point: Bombay, London and Toronto. But when the plane arrived here in London, they caught me because of the forged documents – they didn't allow me to carry on from London to Toronto. In immigration here they ask, 'Where are your original documents?' But if anyone comes with original documents, that means he was never involved in the struggle. If he is involved, he cannot get proper documents!

What happened after that?

They caught me, and I asked to be allowed to go to Toronto. They refused. So I asked for asylum here. But they didn't take any statement from me; they just put me in detention for eight months. They put me in various detention centres, and in prison also: Harmondsworth and Lakshmi House and the [prison] ship – Earl William… I was released after the cyclone – because of the scandal! [The Earl William nearly sank with all the refugees on board in 1987.]

• My house was close to the town, and all the time the army went along the road where my house was. Every time the army used to come to our house and search it and everything. My husband was in Britain on a student visa, and I wanted to join him. I went for an interview at the Embassy in Colombo, and they didn't reply, at least for one year. So I went to India and came straight from there. I came on an open visa, and straightaway told immigration, 'I was waiting for your reply, I didn't receive your reply… After one week they said, 'You go back to your country and get an interview and get a proper visa. Then you can come back.' I said, 'I can't go to my country, there are a lot of problems there! My husband has a student visa, let me stay with him.' My case was taken up by a British man, and a Conservative MP stopped my deportation. I appealed against it; then I got pregnant, and when I was called for an interview I said, 'I can't travel at the moment.' It was postponed, postponed, then my baby was born, and now they have given me a visa, a one-year visa.

• I was supporting the EPRLF, and at the same time I was working with the Citizens' Committee, but the other military groups didn't like my being in the Citizens' Committee and they didn't like my support of the EPRLF. The other groups threatened me, and the EPRLF also asked me to go to India and help them in India, because I'm a skilled worker. So I went there, and I was helping them to make arms. But when the Indian army went into Sri Lanka and started fighting there, I didn't want to support the Indian army, so I had a disagreement with the EPRLF. The EPDP [Eelam People's Democratic Party] broke off from the EPRLF and I went along with it – I was a member of EPDP. After Douglas [Douglas Devananda, leader of the EPDP] was arrested by the Indian government, I had to escape from India… It was very sudden… I came here without a passport, only a Sri Lankan identity card.

• I was a student in Sri Lanka in 1984 – a GCE O Level student – and at that time I supported the Tamil Tigers. I was arrested by the Sri Lanka police and interrogated for five days in a camp. After that I couldn't continue my studies because I was a noted person, so I went to India. While I was studying in India, I supported the Tamil Tigers. Then the Indian army entered Sri Lanka and started fighting the Tigers; after that, Tamil Tigers and Tiger supporters were at risk in India, so I wanted to escape from there too… I didn't have a passport or visa.

What made you decide to leave Sri Lanka?

• The Sri Lankan army, the Indian army, and the militant groups. The Indian army was chasing the people who were involved; the Sri Lankan army was chasing any young, unmarried Tamils: and the groups were chasing everyone to get them to join: if you don't join, they think you are an enemy.

Why did you choose to come to Britain?

Amnesty International invited me to come as a speaker for a meeting they were organising, because they had taken up my case when I was detained. I was arrested in December 1985 by the Sri Lankan army, and detained for two years – at Boosa… I was tortured for about three months until letters were received from England.

Did you come with the idea of staying on?

No I didn't, but I had a problem at the airport in Sri Lanka – I was arrested at the airport. The same day that they arrested me, when they put me in the cell, the JVP blew up the place – it was the day of their jail-break – so everything was in chaos, I lost all my luggage. Earlier I didn't want to stay on in England, but that made me realise it would be dangerous to go back. (R)

• The Tamil population of the East was harassed by all the services, especially the Special Task Force, which was concentrated in Batticaloa. There were numerous incidents where innocent men, women and children were killed either by the army or by the Home Guards. These were not even retaliatory – sometimes it was just for the sake of killing. The day before the TULF leaders came to Colombo in July 1986 for their discussion with J. R. Jayawardene, an army contingent had gone by launch from Trincomalee to Mutur, shot dead 30 men, women and children who were refugees, and there were 30 more who were missing. There was no provocation – nothing whatsoever. This, we felt, was an attempt by the army to sabotage the talks between J.R. and the Tamil leaders.

My eldest son was killed by a gang of thugs at Dehiwela, on the 26th July 1983. What happened was, I was at that time in Batticaloa, a visiting lecturer in English there, and that day of all days, my wife had got it into her head to go to the dental surgery in the hospital to have a tooth extracted. So she had gone earlier. My son was on leave that day, my eldest son. He went towards Wellawatte, saw the houses and shops burning, came back home and waited till about 12 o'clock – his mother hadn't come. So he and my fifth son got into a taxi and went to the hospital.

There was a crowd in front of the hospital. Unfortunately, these fellows were talking Tamil in the taxi. So when they went into the hospital, the taxi driver must have probably tipped off the crowd there – because if you look at my sons, you can never tell that they are Tamil. The eldest son went up, the other was downstairs, then the crowd came up to him and asked him, 'Demala de?' [Are you Tamil?] So he said, 'Ne mamme lansi.' [No, I'm a Burgher.] But since he had spoken in Tamil, they started assaulting him. He tried to defend himself, couldn't do anything, ran this way, that way, ran into a room. They had torn his trousers also – they tried to hold him by the trousers, and when he hit the hand, his trousers tore. Then he ran into one of the wards behind, and those chaps protected him – the Sinhalese chaps. Someone gave him a sarong, he put on the sarong. He was bleeding also – someone had hit him with a stone – so they put a plaster there, on his head, they gave him a covering for his head. They took him by the back door and he got out there, he came out to the bus stand, there were no buses, so he walked all the way back home. He was saved.

Then, at about 12.30, my eldest son was bringing my wife downstairs when some Sinhalese told him, 'Don't go, because they're killing Tamils.' But this fellow didn't bother about it. He went out, went to the bus stop, they were waiting there for a bus but they couldn't get one. My wife was a very bad heart case, so he told his mother, 'Hold on here, I'll just see whether I can get a taxi' – there were one or two taxis there but there was a tremendous crowd.

When he went up there, some people recognised him as the chap who had got out of the taxi. They surrounded him, and I hear one fellow hit him with an aerated water bottle, and he fell unconscious. When my wife tried to go there, there was a Sinhalese woman who held her by the hand. Then when he got up, probably he must have been in a daze, he couldn't have seen his mother, and he started running into the hospital shouting 'Amma, Amma!'. The crowd followed him there and bludgeoned him to death… My wife only heard him shouting 'Amma!' Then this Sinhalese woman dragged my wife on to the canal bank – she was in a shanty, I hear. Because of the curfew, there was no transport. She spent the whole night there. The woman went out to some other hut and brought a roti made out of wheat flour with some sambol and gave it to my wife, and some water to drink – kept her there. Early morning she woke her up at four o'clock and walked her home.

Nobody knew what had happened to my son. So some Sinhalese boys who were friends of my other sons said, 'We'll go and check up.' They went round all the wards: no sign of him. Then they tried to go into the mortuary, but they were refused permission to go in. So they came back and said, 'We were not allowed to go.' My landlord's son was a police inspector, so he said, 'Look, I'll get into my uniform and go there.' So he got into his uniform, went there, saw the body in the mortuary, came back and told my sons. They decided not to tell my wife.

This was the 26th. On the 27th, a crowd came to attack the house. They were warned that the crowd was coming; my wife was in the meantime with some Sinhalese friends at some other place. So my sons jumped over the wall into the next compound; that belonged to an army officer, he kept them there. They came into our house, broke all the furniture, wood and everything, and they left. The army officer said, 'Look, you can't stay here, it's very dangerous for you, the only thing is to get into the refugee camp.' That night they couldn't get a taxi. Early morning by about 5 o'clock, they managed to get a reliable Sinhalese taxi driver to take them to Dehiwela Police Station. From there they were sent to Ratmalana.

There were some 10 or 15 thousand refugees at the airport; and my wife, with a heart condition, not knowing what had happened to our eldest son... Luckily, there was an officer there, a Sinhalese chap, who had known me; he took the eldest of my surviving sons aside and asked, 'What are you doing here?' My son said, 'Look, my eldest brother has been killed; this must not be known to my mother.'

'Yes, yes, I heard that your mother was a heart case; you can't stay here. The only thing to do is, there's a small number of refugees in Mount Lavinia, I'll go there and speak to the warden and we will get you the best accommodation there possible.' He went out in the evening, and next morning they were shifted to Mount Lavinia, and looked after there very well. Then this particular officer arranged for them to come by sea to Trincomalee; they were put on the first possible ship, and they came there on the 8th of August...

In Trincomalee, my second son was working as a clerk in the Urban Council. He lived about 10 miles north of Trinco. On the 22nd of May, 1985, it was, I think, there was an encounter between a Tamil militant group and the navy, in the course of which an air force officer was shot dead. All the navy fellows took cover – this was near the beach. There was an exchange of fire, after which the militants withdrew. The navy fellows remained under cover, and early in the morning they started moving. They shot about six people before coming on to the main road – innocent Tamils.

My son, unfortunately, was waiting at the gate of his house, to catch an early bus to get to work. A fellow with a gun just came and asked him something, put the rifle right on his heart, and fired. He died on the spot. And then, when my daughter-in-law screamed, he pointed the gun at her, so she dragged the two children and ran behind. And then she came back only after about 15 minutes, to find her husband dead. There was no communication with Trinco, so she waited there. When the bus came, the bus driver knew what had happened; he took her into the bus, brought her to Trinco, dropped her there, and she told us – we got the news at about 8 o'clock. But the Sinhalese army officers maintained that when my son was shot, he had a rifle in his hand. Utter lies! The worst (if you'll pardon the language), the worst bloody liars I ever came across!

Two days before that, the army had walked into my house and subjected me to a brutal assault. I was very unpopular with the army, because I had got articles about their activities published in various magazines; so these fellows didn't relish the idea of their violations of human rights being published in magazines. The army policy was this: a good Tamil is a dead Tamil. Nobody was safe at that time.

• I was a witness of a massacre by the government armed forces; the Tigers had killed some soldiers, so in retaliation they killed all these innocent Tamils. I gave the report to the international media. It came to the Ministry, and they issued a warrant to arrest me. I got the news, and I left immediately.

• I was arrested by the Sri Lankan security forces in 1984, February, and I was in prison in Welikada for 21 months. I was tortured terribly: they hung me upside down, they beat me, and forced me to smoke chili powder, and I got wheezing after that. I was unable to walk for three months! My bones were broken due to the beating, my ankle was dislocated due to the hanging, and I lost two of my teeth. They inserted aluminium pipes in my rectum, and it started to bleed. Someone had given the information that I was treating patients from the militant groups. I told them, 'I don't bother to find out if they are militants or civilians.' That was my position. So they said, 'You should know the Tigers (or the insurgents, or the terrorists), and tell the State.' I didn't know, actually – how could I say? So they harassed me and continuously ill-treated me, and ultimately they put me in prison.

According to the Prevention of Terrorism Act, they can't keep a person in detention without trial for more than 18 months, so we started a hunger strike. Though the Prevention of Terrorism Act is a wrong Act, we asked them to implement their own Act – at least that much! That was our demand. So after that, they had to release us; in the meantime, two of the British parliamentarians visited us, and they took our case, and Amnesty International also intervened, so the agitation was more, and they had to release us.

Within 10 days I left Sri Lanka; I didn't even go home, because that was such a terrible period. Some of the victims who were released were shot dead by the army after being released! When this story came to us, we didn't want to go home to our areas. So I went with my wife to India.

How long were you in India?

I was in India for nearly four years. There's an organisation called the Tamil Rehabilitation Organisation – TRO – and I was working with them. It was started in June 1985 by Dr Jayapullarajah – he, myself, and another two or three Sri Lankans, we formed that organisation on a voluntary basis. We got enough funding from Sri Lanka and Europe and so on. Initially we worked in three camps which were close to Madras, and gradually we were able to cover about 85 camps in about four districts. We had a mobile medical unit, and if we started work one day, we used to return after 14-15 days. So the whole day and night we used to visit, giving them medicines, as well as for the children we gave milk powder, and for the elderly people some assistance and nutritional foods; and some clothes too, cooking utensils, things like that. If they were too crowded, we supplied materials and worked to make them some huts.

At the beginning it was terrible; you know, all the people didn't get proper medical attention and they were suffering a lot of diseases – skin diseases, infections – all kinds of things. But gradually, after we started, after six months we were able to observe a marvellous improvement. What we did was to make monthly visits, and in the meantime we had a clinic open daily in Madras, and it was functioning – we appointed some doctors. We also selected some educated youths and girls from the camps and trained them in para-medical work, gave them some first aid kits, and got them to work there. So we were able to reduce disease and improve health conditions. After that, we opened three district clinics in Madurai and Tanjavur, and we were running those. We were doing a good job there!

After the Indian government's agreement with the Sri Lankan government, the Indian government's attitude towards Sri Lankan refugees changed completely: they asked all the refugees who were in camps to return to Sri Lanka, and they sent them back by force. Without the refugees, there was no point working there. In the meantime, they gave some harassment to me also – periodical check-ups and interrogation – and I was afraid of being sent back to Sri Lanka because I personally suffered a lot when I was in prison. So I came to Britain instead – at the airport I went to the immigration officer and said that I want political asylum.

• In 1983, during the violence – the July violence – we were in Colombo – in fact, I was sitting for the LLB examination on that day – and my future wife was a lecturer in the university. When the paper was over, we came out and just saw smoke everywhere – you couldn't even see! And people were running, there were no buses, and the university authorities told us not to go out, so we waited there.

My father, at that time, was the vice-president of the Ceylon Workers' Congress, so we wanted to go to their office, but we couldn't go. So some service boys came, and they brought a car, and they took us there. On the way to the office, from a distance, I saw smoke rising from the building. So I thought, 'They have burned that also'. But when we came in, we saw – inside the premises there was a shop – they had burned that. For five days we stayed there. For the first two days, there were 150 people in the office, and there was no food! There were some children also; Tamils who were walking on the road when the violence started, came to take shelter there. There were some guava trees in the compound, so we managed to get some guavas. And there was a hotel on the other side of the road; some people managed to walk across and get some food. So we managed for two days; after that, food was arranged. But I didn't go home – I was there for about a month, and there were others who stayed for two or three weeks.

At that time, six of my relatives got killed in Nuwara Eliya – one uncle and five cousins, part of two families. This was the only Tamil family in that area, but they had been living there for 100 years. They were very friendly with the Sinhalese, but at that time a big mob came and attacked them.

Did people from the area carry out these attacks, or people from outside?

Always when you enquire about this, they say that people came from outside. This is not always the case; people might have come from outside, but in this case they said the local people also got involved. People came from outside and said they want to know about the area and the people living there, and some local people fell in with them. The mob came in the night and attacked them. So all these things made us decide to leave. We didn't think of leaving permanently – we thought we'd go and stay for some time and then come back.

Our marriage took place because of the violence – like a lot of other marriages! Because we are from different castes, my wife's parents were at first opposed to the marriage; but after the violence her parents thought, 'Now everybody's going to get killed, so they might as well get married!'

• In 1977 my father had a shop in Ratnapura – everything was burned and destroyed. But at that time I was in Jaffna, I didn't have any experience, really – only my parents suffered, we didn't see. In the 1983 riots we saw it with our own eyes. We were staying in Kotahena. All the houses were burned. Actually, we are alive because of our next-door neighbours – Sinhalese on one side and Muslims on the other side.

Tamil houses were being burned?

Yes. After we left, my sister's house was also burned. Then we stayed in the camp for 14 days. We really suffered a lot, because until we went to Jaffna, we didn't know if we were going to be alive! Yes, because any minute… we could hear the bombs and all that. Then my parents gave me the option: either stay at home in Jaffna, or go abroad, but don't stay in Colombo, they're worried because I'm a girl. Then my sister was in Britain, and she called me to come as a student.

I had been working at a bank in Colombo, and I didn't have a passport. I had to get a passport, and for that I had to come to Colombo. The bank gave us two months' leave; then the third month they sent us a red letter saying, 'If you want to come to the office you must come immediately, otherwise we are going to sack you.' Then I came back in September, I came back to my office. I didn't have anywhere to stay – I actually stayed with one of my Sinhalese friends then, because I wanted to get my passport as well. When I came back, we couldn't walk straight on the roads because we were so scared, we were frightened to open our mouths! In public, we would never talk to each other, you see, because then they could pick up our accent and straightaway identify us as Tamils. We really had a hard time!

I stayed in Jaffna for two-and-a-half months, then came and stayed with this Sinhalese friend in Colombo, then somehow or other my Sinhalese friend helped me to get a passport – because I didn't have anybody to sponsor my passport application, so it was difficult. Actually, at the time I left Sri Lanka, I didn't intend to get refugee status. I just wanted to be out of the country for a while, so I came as a student. But then I couldn't go back because the problem was going on and on, so I asked for asylum.

• I was offered a job in Batticaloa, as a consultant, which involved the design and construction of the university complex, and I was very satisfied with it. But then the killing started in that area, and the satisfaction was dead. I accepted that job for 18 months, but within those 18 months there were so many difficulties! The first problem was that our house used to be in front of the main police station, so there was crossfire and various things. Our daughter was only very small at that time, so we had to leave our home and go somewhere else – we never were able to be in peace in that home… I also had to travel 10 miles for work, so on a lot of occasions we were stopped and checked by the security forces… It got to such a state that we couldn't live there any more. They started burning the villages – in the mosque they prayed and then started around 9 o'clock – gunfire and burning, we could see it in the night. They were coming with the help of the government forces, so we had no alternative, we had to go into the jungle, and we were there the whole of the night. And what's more, the next day we didn't get any relief. That was a nightly terror we will always remember! On both sides they were burning houses, Muslims [Home Guards] with the help of the security forces – it was an organised thing, they were not just attacking Tamils, they were chasing them out! That's the real time we decided we can't stay there… [That was in] May 1985, about a week before we left. We had to leave the house and everything behind.

• We had to leave the house and run to the woods, and I had fever there and we couldn't get a doctor. I could see the village burning, and I could hear people saying that my uncles were leaving the town, and I was wondering what's happening. Our daughter was only nine or ten months old and I was feeding her, the dogs were barking and coming towards us, and we were afraid that because the dogs were barking, we would be found. So that's what made us decide to leave the country.

• My husband was a non-commissioned officer in the Sri Lankan Air Force. The trouble started on July 25th 1983. He was on duty, and we were living in Colombo in a rented house. I took my children to school as usual. From the office he realised that the situation was very bad, so he came to the school and fetched me and the children. The whole of Colombo was up in flames. The people were beaten up by servicemen and thugs. He left us at home and went back to work. They passed a curfew through the whole of Sri Lanka.

My landlady was Sinhalese. That evening she came home and told me that I have to leave the place because tonight thugs were coming to attack you all. I said, 'I have no place to go and my husband is not here.' My neighbours were Muslims. I explained my situation to them. They asked me to come and stay there. I took all my important things with me. Around 9 o'clock the mob began to attack the home and to break the things, and they burned a few things. Truckloads of troops passing through were seen encouraging the mobs.

Next day there was no curfew for three hours. I left the children with my neighbours and went to church. I told my situation to the priest: he was a Sinhalese priest. He said, 'Don't wait for your husband; take your children and go to the refugee camp. The mobs were shouting not to give places for Tamils, and if your neighbours hide Tamils, they will be attacked by the mobs.' Then I decided to go to the camp. I asked my neighbour to pass the message to my husband, and reached the camp safely.

On Friday early morning, my husband came to see us. The camp was over-crowded; there was no proper food and many children got diarrhoea. Every day there were three special trains to Jaffna; in one of these trains we went to Jaffna. My husband couldn't come with us because he had to go back to work. When we reached Jaffna the situation was quiet, but later on violence continued unabated. The children were going to school one week, then they closed the schools. We stayed in Jaffna for six months. From there we went to Trincomalee.

The place where we stayed was safe. But after some time, the army got information that Tamil Tigers were hiding in our area. The police station was attacked by Tigers. That day my husband was there; he was telling me, 'Now they've started here also. Innocent people are going to suffer.' Any time they would come home and check everywhere – the army, air force, navy and police – they went around checking all the Tamil houses. The army was the worst. Once they came to my house and checked all my rooms. They found my husband's old uniforms and asked me, 'Where did you get these uniforms?' I said, 'My husband is a serviceman in the air force.' They said, 'No, you are sewing these uniforms for the Tigers.' I said, 'Can't you all see these are old uniforms?'

Then they were asking me about my husband: where he works, what position, I-card number. I told them everything I knew. At once they asked me, 'Does your husband support the Tigers?' I said, 'He is an honourable serviceman.' Then a few minutes later they found the album. They looked at it and asked so many questions about my brothers: 'Where are they? Have they joined the Tigers or gone for training to India?' I said no, and gave all the addresses of my brothers' working places. Whatever they said to me in Sinhalese, I had to answer in Sinhalese. Without warning, any time they would jump into the house. I had to speak the same record to each of them. Once they told me, 'If you don't tell the truth, we are going to kill or rape you.'

When every other day the army came and questioned me, the Tigers started to suspect me; they thought I was giving information about them. But I didn't know who was a Tiger and who was not. When the army came and went, the boys would come and ask me, 'Can we come and stay for two nights behind the well? Why can't your husband give us information about where they keep the weapons?' 'My husband is not here, he is in Colombo. I am staying with my two children without my husband. I went through so many problems and came here; I beg you all, don't come here any more.' There was a temple near my house. In the middle of the night each Tamil family had to leave food for the Tigers in the temple. I also did the same: if I don't cooperate with them, they might do something to my family. I was getting forced by both parties.

At that time my mother was in England. I wrote about my situation to her. On the 27th April 1985 I got a call from my mother that she is arranging for us to come over there. Then we came to England on the 28th of May. My husband wanted to come over here. Before he got married, he signed a contract for 15 years, and in May 1986 the contract expired, so nearly three years he has been without a job. So many people are coming in so many ways, but he doesn't want to come in that way, he wants to come in a genuine way. I have been waiting for four years, and so far he didn't get a chance to come to England. The children need their father. How long are we going to wait like this?

These are all undoubtedly stories of persecution, although the intensity of suffering or degree of danger varies from person to person. Rape was not often mentioned, but I got the impression that fear of it was frequently a factor in the case of women, or those with young daughters.

Fitting together pieces of the jigsaw from the last two chapters, one gets a complex picture of a divided community suffering from *multiple* sources of persecution. Unless this complexity is recognised, it would often be difficult to understand what, exactly, a particular individual is fleeing from.

These cases illustrate the hazards involved in entrusting asylum decisions to officials who (a) are ignorant of the political situation in the countries from which the refugees are fleeing; (b) have never experienced a single day of hardship or danger in their lives; and (c) lack the imagination to put themselves in the place of those whose cases they are judging. By way of example, let us look at the reasons which are sometimes given for deciding that asylum claims are 'bogus':

(1) The refugees have chosen to come abroad rather than taking shelter in 'safe' areas in their own country. If we adopt the popular convention of referring to all areas of Sri Lanka other than the Northern and Eastern Provinces as the 'South', this would mean that, since the war is currently being waged in the North and East, refugees should seek asylum in the South.

As a matter of fact, this is precisely what millions of Tamil refugees have been forced to do, as we will see in a later chapter. But it is worth pointing out that many of the refugees interviewed in Britain, as well as in the camps in Sri Lanka, fled to the North and East in the first place in order to escape from violence in the South. It is therefore a patent absurdity to think of the South as a satisfactory place of safety or refuge for them. Indeed, for some Tamils, the trauma associated with the violence they have experienced in the South is so great that even the war in the North and East is preferable. For example, one man I spoke to on the Yal Devi – the train which once used to go to Jaffna but now stops in Vavuniya – said that his family had fled to the North after the 1983 riots; and although he himself was forced to be in Colombo because of his work, he still felt that his wife and daughter were safer in Jaffna; he preferred to endure the separation, anxiety and hazards of the frequent journeys to visit them, rather than expose them to the risk of being massacred in cold blood in the South.

(2) The refugees have chosen to come to Europe or America rather than seeking asylum in the nearest neighbouring country – in this case India.

Once again, fleeing to India is something which hundreds of thousands of Tamil refugees from Sri Lanka have been forced to do, many living in camps where conditions are comparable to conditions in Sri Lankan camps. It seems to me there is something slightly perverted in the notion that rich European and American countries cannot afford to shelter asylum-seekers whereas poor Third World countries like India can. However, it is not poverty alone which makes India unsuitable for Sri Lankan refugees. From a very early stage in the conflict, the militant groups had bases in India, and many Tamils from Sri Lanka have been killed by them there; so for refugees attempting to escape from any of the militant groups, or to prevent their children being recruited into them, India was never a satisfactory option.

Moreover, India became directly involved in the conflict in 1987, with the signing of the Indo-Lanka Peace Accord and the entry of the IPKF. From then onwards, Sri Lankans opposed to the Indian involvement were no longer safe in India, and there was also general pressure to repatriate refugees to Sri Lanka, by force if necessary. It is once again patently absurd to recommend that refugees fleeing Indian government forces in Sri Lanka should seek asylum in India.

(3) The refugees have come illegally.

This is a typical Catch-22 situation. As some of these cases show (and there are others too), getting asylum from Sri Lanka is to all intents and purposes impossible: I didn't come across a single case of it. Those few asylum seekers who entered legally had come as students or visitors. So all refugees are in effect *forced* to come without a valid entry permit, some after waiting for years. Nor can everyone afford to hang around for so long; those fleeing an arrest warrant or death threat have to leave immediately if they are to have a reasonable chance of survival. For people in such situations, as some of the refugees pointed out, it is often impossible to obtain even a valid passport, much less an entry permit; they are in many cases forced to rely on the numerous agencies which have apparently sprung up to meet this desperate need – supplying, more often than not, forged documents.

The fact that some people come as visitors or students and then claim asylum is also not a reason for doubting their bona fides. Many of the asylum seekers interviewed here had come in the expectation that the situation would change for the better and they would soon be able to return. However, none of those interviewed thought that the situation had improved, and most thought it had deteriorated since they left. I was able to confirm the validity of their assessments in the course of my two visits to Sri Lanka.

A genuine problem does arise in the case of asylum seekers who may have engaged in crimes against civilians in Sri Lanka; indeed, it is evident from some of the foregoing testimony that there are some Tamils who continue to organise such attacks even from Britain. In the case of those who may have committed crimes in Sri Lanka, it is important to remember that they are still, nevertheless, entitled to a fair trial and respect for their own rights, and should not be sent back until these are guaranteed. In the case of those who continue these activities from within Britain, the purpose of stamping out their crimes is certainly not served by treating *all* refugees as criminals; on the contrary, people living in daily fear of deportation are more likely to fall prey to threats, intimidation and violence from within their own community.

In the next chapter we turn to the fate of refugees who succeed in gaining entry to Britain. At this stage it is sufficient to point out that there is no way that asylum claims can be processed efficiently unless they are handled by people who are qualified for the job – i.e., people who have a thorough knowledge of the historical background to the situation they are dealing with, as well as day-to-day current developments. They would not then waste time by asking questions like, 'Why don't you seek asylum in India?' at a time when India had become a party to the conflict and was persecuting and repatriating refugees.

In addition, some training is required to ensure that they understand that even for people inured to suffering, there are limits to human endurance, and to push them beyond these limits is tantamount to violating their human rights. I have lived in conditions of material insecurity and hardship which most people in Britain would find intolerable, and I have known people who live in conditions ten times worse, so I know very well that one can adapt to – live with, make the best of – some fairly dreadful conditions. But I'm very sure that I could never adapt to living in the constant fear that my husband and children could arbitrarily be picked up and tortured to death any time they go out; that someone could enter my home and rape or kill me without fear of punishment; that I and my family and neighbours could at any moment be hacked or burned to death. Could anyone adapt to living with that fear? I don't think so. And it is unethical to expect that anyone should be forced to live in such conditions.

The concept of 'human rights' has arisen precisely because to violate those rights deprives a person of humanity, and to expect a person to live without those rights is inhuman. If people dealing with asylum claims had some training in basic human rights so that they were quite clear about this, they would be able to do their job much more quickly and efficiently; they would not need to spend years deciding the cases of most of the refugees quoted here.

Chapter 3: The experience of exile

Refugees who reach Britain, compared with those remaining in the camps in Sri Lanka, can perhaps be considered lucky: at least their physical distance from the conflict and chances of living a decent life are greater. Yet they too face problems and hardships which make this, in most cases, only a stop-gap solution. The problem causing most anguish, perhaps, is the difficulty of getting asylum, and the consequent insecurity and fear of being sent back. Statements like these were common:

> • We are still on tenterhooks: any time a letter may come asking us to get back to Sri Lanka. We don't have a proper stay – it's a psychological problem.

> • I'm still always scared of being sent back.

> • I keep thinking I can be deported at any time. I can't do any work or studying; I have no peace of mind.

But in some cases the fear was more acute:

> • The reason why I don't feel at home is because I don't feel well at the moment, mentally or physically… After 1985 March, April – that was the beginning of my terror. Before that I felt well. Right now, the situation for me is like I'm at home and every time I see a car pass by, my heart starts beating. Every time a car parks outside my window, I just feel that somebody's come to pick me up.

What happened?

> I had my visa till October 1985. From 1985 March my brother, my whole family, they just cut off from me. And then in October 1985 my money ran out. So I just wrote a letter to the immigration officer. When I wrote the letter I was at one address, and I wrote the letter saying that I'm going to move into another address with some of my friends who are going to put me up because I cannot pay my rent any more in this place, so any further communication should come to me there. And the usual procedure is, the Home Office normally acknowledges the passport, but any extension of visa or your passport coming back, it takes six to eight months.

That's what happened to me the first time – I mean, after the first year. So I was there for seven to eight months expecting a reply to my letter – I mean, I wrote to them: look, I haven't got the money, I cannot go back to my country right now, you know the situation is tense out there, I've lost touch with my family, I don't want to go to the airport and just give myself up to the officials, so what can I do? Since I didn't get any reply after eight months, that's when I got worried. I said, okay now, this officially means that I've been staying in England illegally. The thing is, I did not register the letter which I sent, so you know, that was the beginning of the problem. So I just took off with my bags, and carried on from there, living in several places.

Did they have your passport?

Yes, I sent my passport to them.

But not registered?

My passport was registered; the letter that I wrote was not. I mean, I was not short of money then – I wouldn't have thought about forking out another £1.69 or £2 for a registered letter. It's just that I didn't take it that seriously, I thought that they would receive it anyway.

You never got any response?

No. And that was the beginning of my horror. I just went everywhere, doing odd jobs and paying my rent wherever I went. My friends helped me a lot at that time – my Malaysian friends, guys from the college…

Then they came and arrested me. I was working in a restaurant at that time, and when they arrested me there was nothing I could do. I used to take sleeping tablets – three or four, just to sleep the night. And I used to sleep for something like 26-30 hours, or sometimes I'd just sleep till all I wanted to do is get up. If I had something to eat, I'd eat; otherwise, I'd just go back to sleep again. I was living like that for about two-and-a-half years. And when they arrested me, I thought to myself, okay, the worst has happened to me, and I'll just have to find a way out of this.

Then they put me in a police cell for the first time. I had no lawyer: when they asked me if I wanted a lawyer I said, 'No, I don't want a lawyer,' because I had only three pounds in my pocket. So there was no way out but to say: 'All right, you can send me back, but just get me out of this prison.' You know, I stayed in the police cell eight days – just locked up in one room for eight days – and the only alternative for me to get out of the place or to see some sunlight was to sign and say, 'Okay, I'm going back'. You know, that was my idea, that's the way I thought. And I couldn't hire a lawyer to represent my case because I had no money. And I couldn't get in touch with my family anyway.

When they came, they said, 'Okay, this is your case: by 1985 October you didn't get in touch with us, so that makes you an illegal immigrant for so long: we are deporting you.' So when they said, 'We are deporting you,' there was nothing else I could do. At that time, I didn't tell my political involvement to these people because I thought: I'm not going to give them any information which will make things difficult for me when I get back, you understand. So I just said, 'Okay, fine, if you are going to send me back, send me'. You know, it was like the end of the road for me, practically. So I just signed, and they took me to Harmondsworth detention centre.

That is when I met two Tamil friends there. They said, 'You get in touch with TRAG [Tamil Refugee Action Group] and they'll help you.' I got in touch with TRAG and told them, 'Look, this is my situation.' They said, 'Okay, apply for political asylum, we will back you up.' After two days they took me to Lakshmi House – that's a so-called detention centre, but it's a prison: all prison rules apply there. And when I went there, I saw another 17 Tamils all locked up for similar offences, and that's when I really understood the kind of difficulties the Tamils are facing in Britain. Not that I committed any offence: in their view I have absconded, but at no point did I abscond. I still don't want to do it because I'm not here to make money or anything – I mean, I have no one to send this money to, anyway: my family is much more well-off than I can ever imagine being in this country! So I mean, money is never a problem for me – I don't have to make pennies and send them to my family. But I have fears of persecution back home like all Tamils there, and my family is in danger and everything like that – hopefully they're alive. I just don't want to go back yet.

Anyway, about two months ago, the Home Office finally decided that my political asylum was refused and that they were going to deport me. And my counsellor at UKIAS told me, 'See, they're going to deport you, but we're going to appeal against it.' Anyway, I was in Lakshmi House for about three months, then they released me and said that I should sign with the police station every Monday, which I'm still doing.

So your appeal is being considered?

No, my appeal right is cancelled because when I signed a form in the police station, in effect I signed against my appeal – that's what they're saying now. I am a person who is liable to be deported if and when they wish – any time – so I'm just on a limb, hanging on. And so that has affected me – physically, mentally. Everyone may think I'm a normal-looking guy, but there's nothing in here – it's all gone.

The fate hanging over this refugee has been suffered by many Sri Lankan Tamil refugees. The most celebrated case was that of the five who won the right to apply for political asylum in Britain in July 1989. They had arrived in Britain on different dates between February and June 1987 and applied for asylum; all claimed personal experiences of violence, including periods of detention and the killing of close relatives, and one showed evidence of having undergone torture. Their applications were refused in August and September by means of a notice which stated: 'The Secretary of State, having considered the individual circumstances of your case and in addition the situation in Sri Lanka, has concluded that you have not established a well-founded fear of persecution in Sri Lanka.' (Adjudicator's Determination, Immigration Appeals Tribunal, 13.3.89, p. 3)

The five were deported back to Sri Lanka in February 1988, but their lawyers subsequently lodged an appeal against the rejection of their asylum applications with the adjudicator of the Immigrations Appeals Tribunal, who in March 1989 ruled that all five had a well-founded fear of persecution; at least two had been interrogated and one tortured since being deported; that they had been entitled to political asylum at the time when they were deported, and the Secretary of State's decision was therefore not in accordance with the law; that they were still entitled to political asylum since the situation in Sri Lanka had not substantially changed; and that they should therefore be returned to the UK with the minimum of delay. (Adjudicator's Determination, pp. 25–6.)

However, further delay did follow because the then Home Secretary, Douglas Hurd, appealed against the decision. The High Court ruled that the Home Office had an 'arguable case', and scheduled a judicial review of the Tribunal's findings in mid-July. On 26 July the Court of Appeal upheld the Tribunal's original decision and said the government should pay the cost of their return to Britain. A subsequent attempt by the Home Secretary to suspend the ruling, pending a further appeal, was finally turned down in the

High Court on 31 July. (British Refugee Council, *Sri Lanka Monitor*, May 1989 and July 1989)

Other refugees have been surprised by the treatment they have received in Britain, with its implication that seeking asylum owing to persecution was somehow a crime or offence:

• First they put me in a detention centre for about three weeks. So I had to contact my relations to help me, and two relations signed a surety that they will look after me, they will help me, and they said that they know me well. Then they allowed me temporary admission, and for that they didn't give me proper papers or anything – only the surety paper. But with the surety paper I couldn't get anything from the benefit office – they didn't give me an insurance number for two years. They only called me two months ago and gave me a one-year visa on a piece of paper, because one page of my passport is torn. Because I couldn't get a visa from Sri Lanka – they don't give visas to Tamils – I had to pay some money to an agent, and he did the work to get me from there to here. So he sent me, and the page was torn by him.

I have been to England earlier – I came here as a tourist – so I know about England and everything. I thought, it is a democratic country, according to the law they will help me – that's the reason I came here. But I suffered for about two years.

• When I came here, they say Britain is a democratic state and that and this. But they treated me so badly and put me in prison. I fought over there, but I never went to prison; if they had caught me, if the Sri Lankan army catches anyone in the movement, they always have cyanide capsules, so if they had caught me, I would have died – I was willing to die. I came here without anything, expecting to be better treated, but they put me in prison. And the colour of my skin made a difference to the way I was treated – I had a lot of experience of that in prison.

One of my friends, when he was in prison with me on the prison-ship – the Earl William – they beat him very badly. And they told him, 'If you take any action, we will make things even worse for you.' So he was frightened and didn't take any legal action. Whether it's in a police station or in prison, if they see a white man and me, they treat me differently. I never expected it to be like this here. In Sri Lanka it's obvious – everyone knows the problem is there, a struggle is going on. But here they are always saying, 'There is no problem.' So it's worse here.

Another refugee commented bitterly on the fact that the very circumstance which showed he had no intention of leaving Sri Lanka until forced to do so – lack of a passport – was being used to question the validity of his asylum claim:

Some Tamils have decided to settle down and make their life in Britain; what do you feel about doing this yourself?

> • No, never! Never in my life! I had a chance to leave Sri Lanka since 1975, but I never left – I studied, and got a job, and worked for the people. Only now, because I can't live there, that's the reason why I left. But when I came here, that's the reason why they put me in prison! Because I worked for eight years in a government department, but I didn't get a passport, a Sri Lankan passport. I worked in Colombo, I could easily have got it, but I didn't, because I wasn't thinking of leaving. But here they're asking, 'Why didn't you get a passport?' I didn't want to leave!

The following couple (A is the husband, B the wife), already traumatised by the loss of their home in Sri Lanka, were shocked by the treatment they received in Britain:

What were your major problems after getting to Britain?

> • A: I think the threat of deportation. As a matter of fact, they served a notice to us within one week, for no reason. That is a kind of fanatical thing, I would think – I think they picked up a few people just to show off that they are serious about stopping refugees.
> B: Then we got help to stay on, but that shock was still there.
> A: I was terribly shocked by that. The shock was for two reasons. One is the impression I always had about the UK as highly democratic and human; but that was the biggest shock for me – the way they turned on us. Secondly, the way they reported it on the mass media really, really knocked me down! I think that feeling is still there. Sometimes we feel like getting out – honestly! – but where can we go?
> B: The same problem is there in other countries.

For some refugees, their inability to get family members out to join them is an agonising problem, since they are deprived of the option of going back:

• My wife and children are in India, and I'm missing them. I can't go there because of the boys and the Indian army, so I want asylum in Britain. When I get asylum, I can call my wife and children here. Then, if there's a peaceful settlement, we can go back to our country, Sri Lanka. I don't like to stay here for a long time – I don't like it here. But at least I am safe here!

This woman, having spent four years trying to get a visa for her husband to join her, was on the verge of a breakdown, if not already over the edge:

• Sometimes I hate it very much here… Sometimes I feel like killing my children! You know, my children always hide the knives every day. I get back pain and headaches all the time, so I take pills and all. My son, every day when he goes to school, he'll give me only a few pills and go. He hides the bottle away. Sometimes I tell them, 'You know I had a peaceful life in Sri Lanka, with my husband. Only thing I had some problems with the military and with the Tigers. But after I came here, daily I have to do so many things, I get so tired.' And especially our Sri Lankan people, they always ask, 'Where is her husband? Why isn't her husband coming?' Then they gossip. I don't speak to anybody now. Nobody. Go to church, do the shopping, look after the children, stay at home.

Do you think you will feel all right once you get your husband out?

Yes. But now he doesn't have a job – because he wants to come to Britain, he didn't sign a new contract. So that's a problem, no? Sometimes I send him money – five pounds, ten pounds, like that. I wrote everything – I told them in the last paragraph. The same statement I gave when I came to London, still the same statement I've been giving again and again. This is the last statement, and after this, I'm not going to give any statement. I told my son and daughter that I'm going to hang myself with his pyjama tape. But my son said, 'Mummy, don't you know that nowadays they don't put tape, they put elastic!' Sometimes I talk to myself. So they say, 'You were talking just now'. I say, 'No, I didn't talk.' They say, 'No Mummy, you were talking.' I told them, 'If something happens to me, go to the police commissioner, he'll send you off to Mother Teresa.'

I don't sleep at nights also, every night there is something. If I hear a cat noise even, I will get up and go and see. So when I get up and go to my daughter's room, my daughter thinks I'm coming to kill her. So she says, 'Mummy, Mummy, what are you doing on the stairs?' I say, 'No, I just came to kill you.'

I told them, 'If before this December your Daddy doesn't come...' One of my friends died. So her parents, brother, his wife and two children got visas to come. So I said, 'If I die, your Daddy will come here, your Daddy will get a visa.' So my son said, 'Mummy, you don't die, I will die, then Daddy will come,' he says. So I said, 'One thing: your Daddy must come or I must die before Christmas.'

When it is remembered that these people have already been through traumatic experiences – torture, bereavement, loss of all they possessed, etc. – the extreme cruelty of such treatment is evident. In effect, they are being punished for having been persecuted – a strange notion of justice, but one that is by no means new. Indeed, as an interesting little pamphlet entitled *From the Jews to the Tamils* argues, the attitude of the British authorities towards refugees has remained essentially the same since their hostile treatment of Jewish refugees and political asylum seekers fleeing Nazi Germany:

> The second and main wave of internment came in May 1940... The second wave was the most significant as it manifestly contained the largest numbers of internees who were either the victims of Nazism or the opponents of Nazism or both... In the third week of July 1940, a census was held of the 1500 inmates of one typical men's camp by statisticians interned in the camp. The results are very revealing. 82 per cent of all the men were Jewish... Lafitte also makes it clear that many 'politicals' – communists, trade unionists and other anti-Nazis – were interned... Quite clearly, none of these were allies of Nazi Germany or foes of the British war effort. It is obscene to think they were. In fact the drive for internment came very much from popular anti-semitism and anti-communism, with Jews, socialists, spies and aliens being seen as indistinguishable and all being seen as subversives...
>
> If one looks at the overall history of the treatment of refugees, what is remarkable is the persistence of the myth of free entry existing alongside the reality of restricted or no entry. Indeed every time further controls on asylum seekers are introduced, there is invoked some preceding mythical 'golden period' where British liberalism supposedly welcomed all in danger... Why has all this history been forgotten? ... One explanation is that any revealing of the truth would show Britain's complicity, to a greater or lesser

extent, with those regimes from which refugees are trying to flee. (Cohen 1988, pp. 28–30, 54–5.)

In the understandable anxiety to oppose an Asylum Bill which makes things even worse for refugees, it should not be forgotten, as this quotation points out, that the previous situation was far from ideal. The endless waiting in nerve-racking uncertainty, brutal consignment to detention centres, heart-breaking separation of families – all these could be eliminated by more humane legislation and more efficient processing of claims. The complete impossibility of all travel while waiting for an asylum decision, and the ban on travel to the home country after attaining refugee status, can also cause distress and needs to be reconsidered. It should be understood that one may, for example, be willing to risk one's life to see a dying parent for the last time without necessarily wanting to stay on after the funeral and get detained or killed. Moreover, the possibility of visiting home without being forced to stay on there would actually assist voluntary repatriation, by enabling refugees to find out for themselves whether it is feasible to return without compelling them to burn their bridges in order to do so.

It is important to note, as the quotation above also points out, that refusing asylum to refugees fleeing from a particular situation is not simply a matter of keeping them out, but also involves taking a political stand on that situation. For example, in the case of the five Tamils whose deportation orders were reversed, counsel for the respondent, in requesting the adjudicator to dismiss their appeals, 'strongly urged that Sri Lanka is still a democracy and Tamils were not liable to be persecuted as Tamils' (Adjudicator's Determination, p. 16).

For reasons which have never been publicly explained, the British government has for a long time been taking such a stand with respect to the ethnic conflict in Sri Lanka. During the 1983 riots the British Foreign Office Minister, referring to Sri Lanka, made a similar statement in the House of Commons: 'There is no dictatorship there. There is a thriving democracy, which has a serious problem with its minority.' (Piyadasa 1988, p. 46) This writer comments, 'What was a "thriving democracy" to Mrs Thatcher's government was to Sri Lankans an unprecedented reign of state terror,' and this is indeed the impression one gets from the experiences recounted by the refugees. For anyone who lived through those pogroms or knows what happened in them, the Foreign Office statement is almost like saying that in 1933 the German government was having a problem with its Jewish minority. What problem, one would like to ask? The problem of exterminating them? Presumably Mr Ray Whitney would not have recommended gas chambers as the final solution to this problem?

Given the stand taken by the British government, it is not surprising that some refugees felt that Britain's responsibility for the conflict was not merely historical, as the former colonial power in Sri Lanka, but contemporary, as providing support and help to a Sri Lankan regime engaged in human rights violations:

• Actually, when we come here as refugees, the Sri Lankan government doesn't like it. So what they say, the Home Office also says. The Sri Lankan government says they are economic refugees and all this, so this is what the Home Office also says. So in one way, both are the same – there's no difference, in that way.

• The Western governments have their part to play.

What sort of part do you think they could play?

First of all, let them stop supporting the government that is committing so many human rights violations! They are supplying personnel and ammunition… anti-guerrilla squads, people trained to drive or to pilot their helicopters, and so on.

Which countries, do you know?

As for me, I don't have first-hand information, but people blame Britain too.

For supplying personnel also?

Yes. And when these things are happening, you are keeping bloody silent. When it suits your need, you talk. And when it suits your need equally, you don't talk. Rather than trying to kill the very root, and trace the root and remove it, you say, all right, don't cut. The Western governments don't ask themselves why this is happening. They have to cure the problem there. But instead of treating the cause, they are treating the effect at the airport! That's folly on the part of Western governments.

Would it have any effect if they put pressure on the Sri Lankan government to stop violating human rights?

Certainly! That will go a long way. If these people are sincere about their purpose, if they have real integrity, they can interfere and do something about it. But they don't. It is there where we blame the British government also.

In attempting to find out if there is any basis for the charge that Britain has been supplying ammunition and personnel to the Sri Lankan government at a time when it was known to be committing human rights violations, I came across this account in a pamphlet published by the Tamil Information Centre. I quote from it, complete with references, for anyone who is interested in following up the matter:

> In 1984 the Sri Lankan government hired the Channel Island Company of Kini Meeni Services (KMS) to recruit and train a 900 strong commando unit. (*Financial Times* (UK) 3.9.85) Former British Special Air Services (SAS) personnel provided by the Company have been training the police commandos in alleged counter-insurgency methods. The commandos are now in operation in the Eastern Province, particularly the Batticaloa and Amparai districts, and have proved themselves as the most ruthless killers the island has ever seen. (*The Sunday Times* (UK) 23.2.86) They have killed hundreds of Tamil civilians and burnt thousands of houses and shops belonging to Tamils (Amnesty International Report ASA 37/14/85 of 16.10.85)...
>
> The British government, which said that no sales would be made to states guilty of torture (*Guardian* 9.6.80), has allowed supply of arms to Sri Lanka although evidence of torture has been placed before it by its own member of Parliament (*Sri Lanka: A Nation Dividing*, Robert Kilroy-Silk and Roger Sims)...
>
> It must also be borne in mind that veterans of the former Special Air Services (SAS) (from the Kini Meeni Services) usually do not operate in foreign countries without the tacit approval of the British government. (*India Today* 31.3.86). Furthermore, British pilots have been flying helicopters and airplanes in attacks in Tamil areas and other British mercenaries are reported to be leading ground attacks. The air attacks by the mercenaries have resulted in many civilian deaths and destruction of property. Although this has hitherto been denied by the British government, evidence has been provided by *Times* reporter Simon Winchester who discovered during the first week of May 1986 that two Britons and a South African have been manning helicopter gunships which regularly bomb targets in the Tamil areas. These mercenaries receive a fee of £2,500 a month. (*Sunday Times* (UK) 11.5.86) (Tamil Information Centre, pp. 29, 33–4)

It is this suspicion of collusion between the British and Sri Lankan Governments which accounts for the reluctance of some refugees (like one quoted earlier in this chapter) to reveal to the British authorities information about their political involvements which would in fact support their political asylum claims – the fear being that this information will be passed on to the Sri Lankan authorities and expose them to further repression if and when they are deported back. We have no evidence that this has actually happened, nor that the British government refuses asylum to Tamil refugees because it supports human rights violations in Sri Lanka. However, support of the government which has been committing those atrocities has been substantial, and has taken a variety of forms. Since it is these violations which create the refugees in the first place, it is fair to point out, like the refugee quoted above, that Western governments are treating the effect while ignoring – and perhaps even encouraging – the cause. As another refugee forcefully put it:

> • When the citizenship Act was passed, one million people were made stateless overnight. Who spoke against it? Nobody! And the Western governments, they continued to give aid. If you see, after every act of discrimination, these people have been increasing the aid! Now the government is openly massacring people on a large scale, but still nobody cares, still these Western governments continue to give aid. They must use that to put real pressure on the Sri Lanka government, they must say that 'If you don't respect human rights, then we will not give you aid'. And in the case of the Tamils, when the Tamils started fighting, the Western governments started increasing military aid so much! The British government was giving military aid to Sri Lanka – but they don't admit that, they say, 'We are not involved, private companies are involved.' But of course, for private companies to sell arms to anybody, the government must give them a license! So these things must be stopped.

Solving the problem of refugees from another country is not merely a matter of having decent asylum provisions, although that is an essential part of it. There is also the question of trying to stop the creation of refugees. While there are limits to what can be done from outside, human rights is an international issue, and there are forms of pressure that can be exerted on governments which violate them. However, this requires, first and foremost, that the violations should be acknowledged. Paradoxically, by denying that Tamil refugees have justifiable fears of persecution in Sri Lanka, the British government perpetuates the refugee problem by encouraging the Sri Lankan government to continue the policies that are causing the problem in the first place. In this sense it does have some responsibility for the exodus, and cannot attempt to wash its hands of that responsibility by pretending that it is entirely someone else's problem, or, alternatively, that the problem doesn't even exist.

If there is no fear of persecution, why do hundreds of thousands of Tamils suddenly decide to leave Sri Lanka? The Home Office explanation, apparently, is that they are in search of better jobs and economic prospects. In the case of Sri Lankan refugees, this is really the ultimate irony. Those who have been able to get to Britain are precisely those who come from relatively affluent families in Sri Lanka, most of which own at least their own home, and often additional land as well. The adults among them are mostly well-educated and qualified (skilled workers and upwards), and many have held prestigious jobs in Sri Lanka. To them, one of the features of refugee life causing the most distress is the inability to get work which is in any way commensurate with their previous jobs, and the precipitous fall in status which results:

> • I was an aircraft technician in Air Lanka there, so I was looking for a similar job here; but I tried, I failed, all attempts failed. I left my job when I came, and here also I am not getting a good job.

You haven't got a job now?

> No. I wanted to get into the aircraft field – that may be the problem.

> • I was teaching for 15 years – English as a second language – and I have a teacher's certificate in the English medium. When I came here, I couldn't get a teaching post, so the British Refugee Council helped me to get into Employment Training – it's for one year. During my training I have done an RSA office procedure course. The Royal Society of Arts: it's recognised internationally, so supposing I go to some other country it would still be useful. At the start they said, 'You're an English trained teacher: why should you sit for this exam?' I told them it is because they value the certificates which are given here. Even if you have your degree, PhD, everything from another country, they want their own exam.

What were your major problems in settling in Britain?

• The first thing was to keep myself occupied while I was unemployed. You know, just going to the library, reading the papers, teaching my son... It was something I'd never faced – I had remained very active, you know, all the time. It was a terrible situation. It's not so much the financial consideration, but the fact that you are not employed. The fact that there is nothing to do.

What was your post in Sri Lanka?

I was Deputy Director in one of the Ministries.

How does your present work compare with what you did in Sri Lanka in terms of job satisfaction?

I enjoy doing it, but the amount I can do here compared with what I was doing there – it's about a tenth of what I was doing there! [In terms of the standard of living], I can say I was better off there than here.

• I was a teacher in Sri Lanka... now I'm unemployed. If I were in Sri Lanka, I would be a useful person to other people. So I feel worthless.

• I was employed in the Agrarian Service in Sri Lanka... [Here] I am an ET trainee. From the beginning I found difficulty in getting a good job. First I went to a disco and worked as a porter. Then I worked as a cashier at a petrol pump for four years, but it was closed down, so I came here. I've been working here to make a living, but without any satisfaction.

• I was Senior Assistant Legal Draughtsman – one of the most highly paid government jobs. [Here I am doing] community work with Tamil refugees. I would still like to practise my profession as a lawyer, but because of this racism, I am not able to do that. But I am still hoping to continue. Job satisfaction, until I am able to practise my profession, I won't have. But as somebody who is interested in Tamil and Tamil issues, this work gives me some satisfaction. I am able to serve my community – that satisfaction I have, yes.

But it's more a personal than a professional satisfaction?

Yes, exactly. I'm glad you got the point.

This man's self-confidence had been completely destroyed by the menial nature of his present job compared with his previous one:

> • I have no language barrier or cultural differences or anything. The only thing is, the people here don't recognise our qualifications, even though they are recognised by international standards, and they are not giving proper jobs to us. I can't get a job appropriate to my qualification, which is approved by international standards.

What was your post in Sri Lanka?

> Assistant Archivist – the position was equivalent to Assistant Director in any other government department. At the moment, I am working as a library assistant – that's a very low grade, cleaning books and that and this. Daily I think how I was then, and how I am now; it affects me mentally. Even though 'library assistant' is a minor post, I was holding a big position in my country, because I was managing about 150 staff below me, who were doing the same job which I am doing here now. There I was supervising, but here I'm in the bottom grade.

His wife, who was working as a cashier in a supermarket, confided:

> • He is qualified as a librarian, but still he is working as an assistant. In our country, that is peon's work! All the time he has to see to the books and serve the customers – no peace. Now he is 52 or something; he can't stand all day! He has to work very hard.

Did you have property in Sri Lanka?

> Yes, my dowry house is there, and land also. My house was burned [twice]. The first time was when I was in Colombo. The second time, I heard about it here. My brother-in-law, he took a photograph and sent it to me. It's all burnt, *completely* burnt. Nobody can live there now. It has to be built again.

What were your major problems in settling in?

> Financial problems. In our country there was no problem because my husband was earning enough for us. Now we are both earning, but it is not enough. We applied for a council house, we waited a

long time but we couldn't get it. After that, we decided to go in for this flat – just a two-bedroom flat. There's not enough room: this is the sitting room, we are using it as a bedroom, but there's still not enough room. We have three teenage children. We can't invite anybody because there's not enough space. Only my brothers, sister, brother-in-law – they visit us, but no friends at all.

Have you been losing much sleep over worry?

Yes, definitely! The mortgage problem, you know. Today I checked my bank balance: only £42 there; only 15 days have gone, how can I manage another 15 days? I don't know how to manage. After that the bills come. My husband, he pays only for the mortgage, only for that. Sometimes I even have to get him his travel card. Already there are two bills to be paid; the postman came, and I said, 'Oh no, no!' Sometimes I don't want to open the letter. My husband, he has started drinking, you know. So I can't sleep, thinking, how can I manage? I don't want to borrow more.

• I was Assistant Government Agent [in Sri Lanka]. [Now] I am a book-keeper in a car rental firm… I don't want this job – but I have to exist, I can't commit suicide. It wasn't employment alone, when I was in Sri Lanka; I had a prestigious position there. The people with whom we moved, the status we had in society – we were in a position to help so many people who were in distress!

Did you have any property in Sri Lanka?

Yes – I had a house and some farmland.

Have you been losing much sleep over worry?

Not now, really. I did at the start – in fact I had to take some pills from the doctor for depression… I don't think I'm much use to my family or anyone else… there are so many things beyond our control. My wife's state of mind… she was forced to go out to work to pay for the mortgage. She never went out to work earlier.

• [In Sri Lanka I did] electrical and plumbing work. For the last two months I've been working in a petrol station at the request of the health officer – he wanted to check whether I could work comfortably, because of my health… He wanted me to do some job, to keep myself occupied instead of idling at home. But I would prefer to be doing some other work.

• I was an assistant teacher… I am now a cashier at a petrol pump. It was better in Sri Lanka! I'm trying to get another job, but I couldn't get a good job – so many times I was refused, and the main reason was the language problem, because I had all the other qualifications.

• I was working as a teacher… and am now employed as a cashier at a petrol pump. It's totally different. This is a crazy job!

You haven't been able to find a better job?

I can't find it here, because they first ask about residence, and then I can't get the job. That's why I'd like to go back… How can I go on doing this job? But I have to!

• I was a farmer in Sri Lanka.

Are you employed now?

No. I applied for so many jobs! But I couldn't get anything. I'm still applying, I'm going for an interview, but I don't think I'll get it – I doubt it very much… If I could get a job, it would be all right; but I've tried so many times, and always I've been turned down. I have no hope at all, but still I try… When I don't fulfil my children's needs, that is a big worry. When you're unemployed and dependent, you can't do anything.

• I was (a doctor) running a clinic, until it was destroyed. I'd like to work (here), but the problem is whether the General Medical Council will recognise my degree. I wrote to them, and they sent me a form to fill, and I have sent it; and I have enquired about the exam I have to take.

So you're living on social security?

Yes. But the money I'm getting is not enough for a man to look after himself. The order is that within six months we shouldn't try for any job. So the income is not enough, neither can I go for a job – that's a problem, supporting myself.

The other problem is that I have a family – I have a small kid who is not even three years and my wife – they are suffering in India… Today also I received a letter that the police went and harassed them. So this is a problem for me. Financially I am not in a good position to bring them here, and to get permission also it's a problem.

• When I came here, I was unemployed, I had to depend on others, and I was always thinking, 'I am borrowing something from others,' you see. Because before coming here, I was working for nearly eight years, and earned money of my own. After eight years if you become dependent on somebody, it's very, very difficult. That was my main problem.

• I was a civil servant. I worked in thc office, and I was one of the district secretaries in the union. We worked with the workers and enjoyed ourselves; it was a happy life! But here, we can't get any decent jobs. Only, if I want to, I can get a job in a petrol station or in Kentucky Chicken! We have certificates, but we can't get jobs.

Are you getting social security?

No, now I'm working for two days a week. For the moment I'm working part-time as a night cashier in a petrol station. I don't like it, but there is no other way to live!

• I was a chemical engineer… Actually, I've had a lot of difficulty trying to get a job – they only take into account experience from here. I've had a lot of experience in Sri Lanka, but they don't count that.

• I was a turner in a turning workshop. I also know welding and fitting.

Would you like to get a job?

Yes – but I haven't got a National Insurance number. Friends are supporting me. If the situation in Sri Lanka is peaceful, I would like to return. I can work and earn my living there.

The idea that all these people with a comfortable standard of living in Sri Lanka, and sometimes with prestigious, high-status jobs too, should come to Britain *voluntarily* in order to be unemployed, or to do unskilled jobs in petrol stations, shops or other workplaces, is grotesque. The media as well as the politicians who repeat this story ad nauseam are either shamefully ignorant ('shamefully' because they ought to make sure they are better informed before making statements in public), or even more shamefully dishonest, spreading untruths which they know will be used as a pretext for vicious attacks on helpless people.

This is not to imply that there is anything wrong in coming to Britain in search of employment or economic security. But the fact is that for Sri Lankan refugees, the very opposite is the case: most of them come to Britain *leaving* employment, property, status and economic security because their lives are at risk, and the allegation that they are economic migrants who have left their country voluntarily must be exposed for the contemptible lie that it is.

Apart from the disabilities they suffer as refugees, there are also the problems shared with many immigrants: racism, loneliness, alienation, homesickness, and nostalgia for their former way of life. One or two of the refugees, who had come to Britain very young, thought they might find it difficult to readjust to life in Sri Lanka, especially after the devastating changes wrought by the war:

What do you feel about settling down in Britain?

> • Well, I'm used to things here, and I wouldn't mind settling down here. I still want to go back, but one thing that's against that is that it's not the same as before – all my relatives and everyone, they've become refugees, and everyone's gone all over the place. The rest of my family are here. Nobody has remained in Sri Lanka. Even by the time we were leaving Jaffna and going back to Colombo, by that time half the buildings had gone anyway, and the place was already being transformed. And my uncle, last year, he took some photographs and sent us, and my mum's house – that's been sort of blown in.

This is an understandable response, and the number of people in this category can be expected to increase as the conflict drags on and children who came over with their parents grow up in Britain. Unless normality can be restored in Sri Lanka before they adjust completely to life in the host country, the ideal solution for them is to remain.

There is also the possibility that refugees are too traumatised by their experiences in Sri Lanka ever to wish to go back:

Some Tamils have decided to settle down and make their life in Britain: what do you feel about doing this yourself?

> • It depends on the individuals, no? People like us can't settle down. We can stay for a short time, till the children are settled. When we ask our children, they don't like to go to our country or any other country; they are used to this environment because they were small when they came, they've got used to the set-up of this country. So for them, this is their home, we can't uproot them. Till they are educated and settled, it's our duty to look after them. But after that, we prefer to go to some other country.

Back to Sri Lanka?

> Not to Sri Lanka! I'll never stay in Sri Lanka – such a disgusting place! Sri Lanka is out from my life! I'll never, never go back.

For such people, settlement in Britain or a third country is the obvious solution. But the overwhelming majority of those I interviewed – including young people, including some who had suffered horrific experiences – expressed a desire to go back if peace was restored and they had homes and jobs to return to. For some, this desire was related to negative experiences suffered in Britain, but many who had no complaints about their host country still preferred their own.

Would you think of remaining permanently in Britain?

> • Till the problem is solved in Sri Lanka. If it's normal, if it's all right, I prefer my own country. Nothing like your own country.

Do you feel at home in Britain?

> • No. We don't get any help from others, from people around – we have to find solutions for our own problems. If the situation settles down, it is better to go back; but if it takes five or ten years, then after that it is very difficult for our children to go back and live there. For myself, I'd prefer to go back, but for our children, it's different.

> • If our problem, our minority problem, is settled to the satisfaction of everybody, then I don't mind going back. It's not a matter of minding – I would actually prefer to go back. Here you are on your own, you know; you're not known to your next-door neighbour, and

you are by yourself. But that is not the case there – there we have all our contacts and social life, when you walk in the neighbourhood you know everybody. You are lost in this place – you are to yourself.

Do you feel at home in Britain now?

• No, not really.

What prevents you from feeling at home?

Racism; people passing in cars, they call you 'black bastard' and 'Paki' and all that – I've been called that when I walk along the pavement by a crowd of white hooligans. And your neighbours don't communicate with you in this country.

Would you like to go back to Sri Lanka?

Some time or other I would – if things get better and we are quite convinced that there is no fear of persecution or fear for your life or freedom.

• Economically for me, in my country, I worked for a government department, my wife worked for the department, I had land, I had a profession, and I was maintaining a car there, you know – quite a high standard of living. For my personal field, it is very difficult to find a job in London – it is related to tropical countries like Sri Lanka, you know, nothing to do with countries like Britain. And the environment outside my home, you know – I never get any sort of a feeling that it's like Sri Lanka. I don't know who is my neighbour, and also *they* don't want me to know who is living next door. Enjoying our social and cultural life – it is very difficult here. I feel I must, I want to die in my country.

• One important factor was that when we shifted to London, my son was mugged. It was a terrible thing I went through! He was very small at that time – about ten years. Children younger than him assaulted him. He had a head injury and had to be taken to hospital. It was terrible, you know – from the frying pan into the fire!

What do you feel about settling down permanently in Britain?

Not me; no way! If the violence ends, I'm back. That is one condition: if there is no violence, I am going. Nobody can stop me!

• It's very difficult to make close friends in this country – you can make friends, but not close friends – and I have no relatives here, so I feel alone. I'd like to see my grandma, she's now 80, 85 – I don't know. My mother died in 1983, so my grandma was looking after me, and she likes me very much. Recently she sent me a photo, and she's very ill now – actually, she's going to die.

So she wants to see you before she dies?

Yes. I'm just writing, 'I'm coming, I'm coming,' but I can't go, I know I can't go. And my elder sister, she's a widow, and she's also like my mum, because my mum died in 1983, she came and looked after everything.

So she also would like to see you?

No! She says, 'Wherever you live, that you're alive is enough for us; don't come back.' But *I'd* like to see her.

Will you ever go back and live in Sri Lanka?

If the situation is all right, after some time I'll go. I can get a better job there than I can get here, I can look after our things and live with my own relatives – that's the greatest thing you can get in the world. But in this country… nothing!

• In Sri Lanka, when we have free time, we can go to neighbours and speak to them; but here we can't go to neighbours – we don't even know who they are! … [I feel] lonely because I don't have relations here either.

• Even today we are facing racial harassment problems in this country; still we are thinking that Sri Lanka is the best country in the world.

What kind of problems?

Even when I walk along the roadside without doing any harm to others, when passing people see me, they call out 'Paki' and all those things. When you see an advertisement, when you call over the telephone, immediately they tell you that vacancy is filled. From the accent – because they didn't ask my qualifications, they didn't ask my experience, they didn't ask my age; from the first word, they say that it is filled. But the next day, next week, the advertisement goes on.

The Asians get problems from both sides – from blacks and whites… In Sri Lanka the racial discrimination is created by the politicians. I was born in a Sinhala district, and I lived there; most of the people, they are okay. This is an organised problem in Sri Lanka. But here no one is organising, but in spite of that you can see it in the public.

You think it's worse here?

Worse here. I think anyway one day the Sri Lanka problem should be settled and we can make it into a paradise.

• If I could [return to Sri Lanka], I would. That's the only thing I want to do right now – there's nothing more I want in this life: just to go back, come back to normality, I mean. In spite of the discrimination I've faced in that country, Sri Lanka is still my own country.

• I'm not satisfied because of the racial harassment [in Britain], and also because I haven't got any proper employment. I would like to return back to my country, but not now.

• If there's no problem, I would like to go back to Sri Lanka. But I don't like to go there when there's trouble. When we came, we just wanted to avoid the problems there, so we came here. If there's peace there, we want to get back. I don't say that this life here is bad, or the people or the climate or the country is bad. But I prefer my own country. Not that I hate this place, but I prefer my own.

• I still want to go back. I came here because of the security problem, but I have to go back because my parents are alone.

• I feel very small to be in this country. Very often I think, with my first degree and legal qualification, I was something there. Until 1977 when this discrimination came to a height, you know, I could contact any of the ministers over the phone. My dealings were always with ministers, ministries. But having lived such an influential life, remaining a person of consequence, to be nobody here! After my LLM, I passed my solicitor's examination, and I had faced these few interviews to be chosen as a solicitor in English firms or in the CPS – that is, the Crown Prosecution Service. We are treated as dust! Whereas somebody here – just anybody from any of the universities – is wanted, I am not.

Even when I was practising my profession, I was lecturing in law at universities, polytechnic, law college, Bankers' Institute, so lecturing had become my field. But after I came here, I applied even for part-time jobs as a law lecturer: not possible. This is disgraceful! It's dehumanising for me, you know. So many qualified people have worked at petrol sheds. I haven't. I would choose to reduce my premiums to one rather than working like that.

Of course, there's also discrimination in Sri Lanka, not only between Sinhalese and Tamils, but also among Sinhalese and among Tamils.

Over there, perhaps because we didn't belong to the downtrodden, we did not experience the humiliation and we did not know what it was. What I'm trying to say is, what humiliation is, we did not know, or rather I did not know when I was in Sri Lanka, because I was supposed to have been born in a higher caste. But when I came here, and assumed the role of the downtrodden here, I started fuming and fulminating. But if you ask me to *compare*, I am sorry, I am not able to compare it because I never experienced it there. But I am experiencing it here!

You mean you feel that you are treated like a lower caste person over here?

Right. That's right. Exactly… There, maybe I deserved 70%, but I was given 60%; here I may deserve 50%, but I am not given even 15%! So in Sri Lanka I was given at least *something* that I deserved. Here I am given nothing.

• Because of my political and social involvement, I don't see much difficulty in settling in. It's okay for the time being. But I'm not thinking of settling here for ever… I want to go and settle there in my country. That's my country; no racial harassment, nothing will be there if we settle the matter. Because it is true that Sri Lanka is a paradise!

• I think in Britain, because a large number of Asians are here, everything is provided according to our likes – I think so. One thing we don't like: the structure of British life is different from the structure of our Asian life. The community life is very different. Here you don't know what is happening in the next house. You are isolated. We like to mix with neighbours, but that is not a part of life in Britain.

• When I stepped in here, I never asked for asylum. Those days, it was not a problem: had I told my whole story, they would definitely have given me asylum, and had I brought my family, they would also have got asylum. But I didn't want to be a political refugee, so I applied for leave, six months' leave, and on the leave I came, thinking that after six months I could go back; and I really wanted to go back. But I found that I couldn't.

My major problem is actually that my children find it difficult to adapt to being here. My elder son got educated in the Tamil medium; now he is sitting for the GCSE, and it gives me pain to see the difficulties he is undergoing, in switching from the Tamil to the English medium. My wife doesn't know much English; after her cultural background over there, she finds it very uncomfortable to be here. More than anything else, I couldn't get suitable employment here!

What do you feel about settling down in Britain?

I'd prefer it if we could go back to Sri Lanka, if the situation and the climate there are more convenient for us, if it is suitable for us to go back – I mean, not coming back to normal, but at least coming back to near normal… My problem is, I may be singled out… I could easily be identified.

• I feel terribly homesick, because I have never gone back since I came to this country. We are not used to this type of living, you see, we are used to the set-up in our country.

Are there any specific aspects of life there which you miss?

Mainly maybe the social set-up. Because we were holding good posts there, so people came to see us and discuss matters. [We are] more isolated here, yes… Even if I had any amount of money, I wouldn't like to stay here.

• Actually, in Sri Lanka I was a housewife, and here I have to work outside; I get tired, but I have to do it. I don't want to take even one day's leave, because it is less money in the bank – they pay by the day… I am a cashier in a supermarket. I need the money, otherwise we can't live. My husband doesn't earn enough, so I must work – I *must* work. My children are still young – they are not working yet. I prefer to be a housewife, but in this country, I can't afford to stay at home.

• Because of the weather and the comfort, everything in Sri Lanka is better. I don't like this country, actually. This is not a happy life; it's a working life, a 'machine life'. Sometimes I think, there's no point in living. Every day is just the same. But it can't be helped… Here, there's no time at all – no time. If I finish at work, then I have work at home, and then I feel tired.

We'd like to go back. If everything is okay, we'd like to go back. I thought that our country has a lot of problems; but after I came here, I realised there are more problems here!

• I wouldn't like to settle in Britain, because I like my country. The political problem is the main thing for me. Here the way of living is different, because they don't get together. In Sri Lanka, suppose if something happens to the next-door people, we will go. And they will say 'Hello,' and get together at least. But here it's entirely different. They will live on their own, everything is through the telephone… We can't leave the children on their own at home. I don't like it. So if the children's education is finished, we can go back, if the political problem is solved.

• It's not my home! It's quite a different environment… maybe the weather… And the treatment we get from these people also is very different from the treatment we get from our people; in your country, the respect that you get is quite different from the respect that you get here. Here, you are just a doctor in the ward, and when you come out, you are nowhere. There, even out in society you are a doctor.

Settle in Britain? I won't do that. I'll be going back if the situation in Sri Lanka is all right. At work you experience (racism) day to day, you know, you realise that you are looked at differently.

You mean, the way they talk to you and treat you?

That's right. Not everybody, but there are people like that… We feel more uncomfortable over here. Over there, even though there is discrimination, we feel it is our home, you know.

• Here we're not actually living, we're only existing. Every day we get up, go to work, get back home, cooking, washing… There, in our place, we were really *enjoying* life – we had time to enjoy life!

• I'm used to living in my own country, the country of my birth, and I don't feel that this is my home country. It's very different here – the culture and everything. I am connected with my country and with my people. And the climate, weather – the climate also is so different.

Are you planning to make a visit home?

Only when all the problems are solved. Otherwise I can't: if I go, they will arrest me. Actually, I want to see my mum, my mum and sisters. I have two nephews and five or six nieces, so sometimes I miss them, I want to see them. But I can't go now because I'm afraid for my life… I don't think I can go for some years. But after that, I'll go back.

• For work, it's okay, but my mind is not happy, it's really not happy. How can I feel happy? My parents, my brother and sister are all struggling in that place. I can't feel at home in this country.

Did you come with the intention of staying in Britain?

No – I just wanted to save my life… But I'm not happy here; I'd like to go back, if all the problems are solved.

• I have experienced racism from some of the people at work – not all of them, but some… We are better in Sri Lanka. Because it is our motherland, our own country. We were living a peaceful life there, before all these problems… At the moment, we *can't* go back to Sri Lanka – not that we don't like to. That is the reason we don't want to go back there now.

• The main problem was my children's studies – that was the first thing, the language… There is the money problem… Everything's a problem in this country, no? … My God, I miss Sri Lanka! Here I

have to work so hard. Before, in Sri Lanka, I was not employed –
there was no need for it. But here I have to go out to work, look after
the children, do the cooking and everything. There's too much work!
I go to the factory at 7.30 in the morning. I come back at 4.30. After
I come back, I have to do the cooking and everything. Sometimes I
get fed up! Sometimes I fight with the children because I'm so tired.

How long did you think you would stay in Britain?

First and foremost, I wanted to look after my children. If I stayed in
Sri Lanka, my children could have problems – they might even die,
no? Sometimes the bombs came through the roof into somebody's
house. I wanted to save my children's lives, so I came here. But
when their studies finish, I go back.

Even if they want to stay, will you go back?

The children may stay here, but I won't stay here! I want to go back
even if the children stay… If everything is good, it's better to go
back, no? I don't like this hard life.

• I don't like this life! … All the work we have to do, all the work;
even when I'm not well, there's no one to help me – I still have to
do all the work all the time. When I'm pregnant like this I feel very
homesick, I feel my home is much better.

I go to work early in the morning, I start from here at 7 o'clock
taking my baby, I drop the baby at another house, then I take two
buses, then I'm at work till 3 o'clock, then I wait for buses again,
get back at 4 o'clock, get the baby, do the shopping, cooking… it's
very difficult. I don't like to settle down here. When the problem in
our country is solved, when a peaceful time comes, then we'll go
back.

What if your children grow up here and don't want to go back?

I'm teaching them from now, that this is not our country, we come
from a different country. I show my baby photos of his grandmother,
grandfather, uncle, aunty – because he knows nothing, only mother
and father!

• Everywhere – in school, on the road, in the house, shops – we get
racial harassment, breaking into the house, thefts, all the time – and

my wife is sick continuously. My children have a lot of harassment even at school. My eldest son was threatened at knife-point thrice, coming home from school, and my third son was robbed just in front of the house: both of us were sick, he went shopping, and at the bus stop he was robbed…

We're living in a black area, so it's mostly blacks here. Then I sent my eldest son to school in a white area, and there it's even worse! So the situation is very bad… In Sri Lanka the discrimination was formed by the politicians, not by the community… If everything is settled in Sri Lanka, I will take the first flight back. Even my daughter always pleads with me to send her back to Sri Lanka; all the time she insists 'I want to go back.'

What are the main factors that prevent you from feeling at home?

No stay, racial harassment, healthwise everybody's suffering, then we're suffering mentally, the children are not free to do anything – they are not free in school, on outings, shopping – they are like caged birds! Wherever you live, you must have peace in life, that is important. But we don't get any at all. Only we have got government accommodation and money – we must be grateful for that, at least we are getting something. But when your mind is not at peace, everything seems wrong. We are alive, anyway; there are so many people struggling to save their lives in one way or another.

• Whenever I go home, my wife immediately starts, 'Why can't we go, at least to India?'… Mainly we miss our friends and relatives. If you're in Sri Lanka, you know that in the evenings you can simply walk out and go into any other house without telling anybody beforehand. Or evenings you can go for films, you can go to the temple – there are so many things! Those are the things we miss – social activities, contact with other people. When you work here, you really have to work! You have no time for social activities – there is nothing called leisure. You have to do the cooking and all those things. My wife goes out to work in the evenings, and also works at weekends, Saturdays and Sundays, so I have learned to cook after coming here – that is one good thing, at least!

• I'm missing my parents – that's the main factor. And it's a different environment… If Sri Lanka comes back to normal, and everything is the same as it was before 1977 – because 1958 I can't remember, only my parents can remember, but before 1977, Colombo and

Jaffna were quite all right, we were quite settled. If it goes back to being like that, we would like to go back – one day, I would like to go back and settle, I'll be very happy to go back and settle if the country is normal.

You'd prefer to go back to Sri Lanka?

• Yes, of course. But not in the climate at the moment… If the conditions are better, if there's peace – and I'm talking about the days which we had before.

What I always wanted is to contribute to that place, but not at the moment. Because I always thought that we have a duty to try to contribute something; that is one reason. And our roots are there, our people are there. My feeling is, if the climate is good, I always want to go back and do something as a way of contributing. I can't contribute by violence or in a violent climate. But if things are all right, then I can do something.

• I have got two little daughters, I would like to go back if there is peace. If there is no peace, if there is no luck, we have to stay here. But if there is peace in Sri Lanka, we have to go because it is better for our children there. I would prefer not to stay here because of the cultural difference.

• I had a problem when I came here in 1986, when I stayed with my sister – she's also a refugee. Her two children, a girl and a boy, and my mother, they came in 1985, in the open visa time. First they stayed in a bed-and-breakfast hotel, after that they got a four-bedroom flat in a lovely block of flats, but they had a lot of racial harassment. Children used to come and bang on the door, they threw dirty nappies and dog-shit through the letter box. They called us 'Paki' and 'you bloody bitch', and asked my mother to 'get out, you old bitch.' They would draw dirty pictures – vulgar – and throw them through the letter box. When we went out, they would splash water on us, they spat on us and threw beer cans. And for a Christmas gift they would put dirty things in a sack and leave it in front of the door.

My children were frightened, so I thought I couldn't stay there, and I went to the housing association and told them about it. They asked, 'Do you think you would like to stay in temporary accommodation?' I thought it doesn't matter, it's better than living with racial harassment, with the children being depressed all the time. So I came to temporary accommodation.

But my sister thought, 'If I stay here, at least they will get me a home,' but they didn't, and for three years she had racial harassment. Every time the CID and the police officer used to come and ask, 'Do you know who the people are, giving you trouble?' And my mother said, 'No, we don't know.' But the policemen, they know who the people are, giving trouble to them. At last my mother said to them, 'If you don't give us good accommodation, we are going to commit suicide, me and my daughter and my grandchildren.' That is the last word she said. Within two months, they gave them a house.

Racialism is the worst thing in this country... The racial harassment here is worse [than in Sri Lanka], because they say in front of people, 'We are giving equal opportunities', but in their mind it's different.

Perhaps it is difficult for people who have lived all their lives in Britain to understand the intense nostalgia and longing for their homeland felt by people who have been accustomed to a warmer geographical and social climate; to understand that it can be a sad, lonely, frightening experience, which can be turned into an absolutely hellish nightmare by racial harassment. But all human beings have the capacity for exercising some imagination; and it should not be impossible for most people to get at least a vague idea of the predicament of these unhappy exiles, forced out of their homes and living in a country where they are uncomfortable, if not positively miserable.

What makes this effort of imagination impossible is the constant propagation of blatantly distorted images of refugees by racist politicians and the media; propaganda which portrays them as economic migrants coming West to seek their fortunes. The truth, as we have seen, is the opposite: these people have been compelled to come, simply in order to save their own lives or those of their children. And there are many others who feel that exile is literally a fate worse than death. Most refugees had relatives or friends, especially elderly ones, who refused to leave Sri Lanka even when they had the opportunity to do so, for reasons like this:

• Some people, you know, they love their country so much, they don't like to go to another country.

• They know it's a dangerous life, but they don't like to come to other countries and be like me: no permanent residence. They would have to sell their property to come here, and then if they can't settle down, that is again a difficult situation for them. So they don't want to come out, they just adjust themselves to stay there.

• One of my cousins is there – he doesn't like to come out. He knows that his life is at risk, but his parents are there, and he doesn't want to leave them.

• Some people are devoted to the land, they are attached to the soil. A lot of parents I know, after coming here they complain, they want to go back.

• They don't like to leave the country because they don't like western culture. They were brought up in the rural areas, the village, so they only like that culture. And they have some property, so they don't like to leave it.

• There is a family who had two sons killed by the army, but the parents don't want to go anywhere. They said, if they die, they will die at home. They don't want to save their own lives by going to another country, because they are mourning for their sons whom they have lost.

• They think that organising life in other countries is very difficult. And here they'll have to wear a lot of clothes – coats and caps and gloves and all that. They don't need that in Sri Lanka.

• So many old people want to live there – they don't want to come here because they can't adapt to a different way of life, and they don't want to leave their property.

• A lot of people, because they were born there, they want to die there. Yes, I have some friends, relations, everybody. They want to live in their country, and even if there's any problem, they want to die there. They don't mind about their lives, because they don't want to die in another country.

• Not because he thinks it's safe to stay there; but he's very strongly attached to the country, he just feels that whatever happens, he will live or die in Sri Lanka – it's his principles. Also, over there he enjoys a certain status: everybody respects him, everybody knows him. He can't get that anywhere else – now he's too old to work up to that status.

• They are risking their lives and staying there, to try to find a solution to the problems.

• The risk is there, the danger is there. But I know my mother is one who simply cannot manage here. She would rather starve and die there than come and get humiliated and bored here.

• They want to stay because they really want to liberate the country, solve the problems once and for all, and live there peacefully.

• They don't understand British culture; they don't understand English. Once we go to work, they just have to put the TV on and watch it, and even then, they can't understand it. So what they think is, let us die on our own soil. That is what they want. Especially old people. They think that staying here is the same as dying there. For example, my wife's sister's mother-in-law: she was here, but she went back and now she's there. Even with all the risk. Because they want to settle down and die on their own soil.

• I know a lot of people who don't want to leave Sri Lanka. For example, one of my cousins. All his children are outside Sri Lanka, they are in Canada and other places, but he doesn't want to go. He says, 'If all the Tamils die, I may as well die too.' He is at risk, his house was bombed, but he feels more uncomfortable to change his environment and undergo a different type of hardship.

• I had a close friend who had full refugee status here, but he went back and got killed. He went back because he thought he could serve the Tamil community better from there than from here.

• My mother doesn't want to live here, she wants to go and settle there. She likes it there, she likes the country and everything. But the problem is she's alone, she can't manage. The police, the army, when these violent people come, she can't run, she can't walk without support – she's a diabetic patient. But she wants to go there.

• The main reason is, they don't want to leave their property, and they're old; some people think, 'We can't come and live in this country because it's cold.'

• Their lives are at risk, but they want to meet the challenge, they don't want to run away from problems.

• I know two doctors still working in the hospital in Jaffna, even though they have the opportunity to come out; this just shows their determination and courage to help the people.

• One of my uncles didn't want to leave. He's dead now – the Tigers killed him. They just came to his home and took him away.

• Often young people leave the country, but older people stay behind. They feel that to settle down in another country is very difficult, that they have to start everything again.

• All my family doesn't want to leave – they'd rather face the situation there than lose their dignity and status and identity.

• They love their country, they don't want to leave the country. It was the same with me, but I had to leave.

And so on, and so forth. To most people in Britain, if they have heard of Sri Lanka at all, it is a place producing tea and a tourist spot. But for those of us born and brought up there, it is a homeland where the love and warmth of relatives, neighbours and friends is experienced against a background of breath-taking natural beauty. Exile from such a homeland is understandably a painful experience.

No insult to Britain, but let us be clear that it is not exactly a paradise – not even to the majority of its indigenous population. People forced to come to it due to circumstances beyond their control need the utmost sympathy and support in order to make life tolerable even in the short term. The last thing they need is racist politicians and tabloids scapegoating them for all the economic, political and social shortcomings of the host country ('Immigration – this threat to our society' etc.), and implicitly inciting fascist gangs to terrorise, assault or kill them.

The ill-treatment of refugees in countries like Britain, is, of course, an expression of their own social crisis; but it also contributes to a deepening of that crisis by diverting attention from its real causes, proposing illusory solutions (as though harsher asylum laws will do anything to pull Britain out of the recession, create full employment, house the homeless, eliminate poverty, etc, etc!), and accelerating the descent into irrational violence and brutality. Greater understanding of the problems faced by refugees and attempts to provide them with asylum and make them feel at home can enable them to make a creative contribution to the country where they have taken refuge. It would also, of course, make their exile more bearable.

However, for most of them this would still be only a temporary or second-best solution; the longing to return would remain. So a further step, for those concerned about refugees, would be to put pressure on those who are creating the refugee problem – in this case mainly the Sri Lankan government, and to a great extent also the LTTE – to cease their human rights violations, which are forcing people to flee and preventing refugees from returning voluntarily. To the extent that human rights are a legitimate concern of the international community,

> It is becoming increasingly clear that the view that refugee movements pose humanitarian problems marginal to the central issues of war and peace, or that they are unique and isolated events, must be superseded by a serious consideration of refugee problems as an integral part of international politics and relations. (Loescher and Monahan 1990, p. 2)

Chapter 4: 'How can we live like this?'

The condition of Tamil refugees in Britain leaves much to be desired; but the state of those remaining in Sri Lanka is incomparably worse. I did not visit Tamil refugee camps in the North and East, and therefore did not see the worst; but what I saw was quite bad enough. Refugees were herded into large halls, their mats spread side by side along the walls and down the middle, all their belongings crammed into that small strip of space which, for the time being, they could call their own. Or crowded into small cadjan [coconut palm leaf] huts, several families in one room.

Facilities were minimal: about four water taps and the same number of toilets shared between roughly 1,500 people; in some camps, people stayed up all night, waiting to use the toilets. Rations – mainly rice and bread – were provided by the government. Conditions had deteriorated between my visits in October 1990 and September 1991, with more and more refugees coming in. Unregistered inmates outnumbered registered ones by about three to one, and since the government provided rations only for those who were registered, the shortfall was made good partly by donations from voluntary organisations, partly by watering down and stretching out whatever food was available, making the monotonous diet even less nutritious and more unappetising. Lacking employment and therefore money, most of the refugees spent their time in forced inactivity, although efforts made by voluntary groups had secured school places for children of school-going age, and later on, classes for pre-school children as well.

Most of these people had fled the renewed outbreak of war in June 1990. One woman in her late twenties had come from Batticaloa in early June for St Anthony's Festival, and couldn't return because the war broke out. When she went back in August to fetch her two little sons, she found that her whole house had been looted, the roofing removed, and so forth. She was worried about the children's schooling, because she had no money for the bus fare to take them to school. Weren't there any teachers in the camp? Yes, there were two, she herself was one. Couldn't they teach children at the camp itself? They had to register at state schools, otherwise they wouldn't get paid. Another worry was that one of the children was ill; a doctor who visited the camp had prescribed some medicines, but she didn't have any money to buy them. I asked how the trouble had started:

> • The recent trouble started only after the attack on the Muslims in the mosque [by the Tigers].

Would you like to go back and live in Batticaloa?

We can't live in our house again unless we are given the money to repair it.

Do you think Sinhalese and Tamils can ever live peacefully together?

I should hope so! My husband is Sinhalese! (General laughter from those around. I later discovered that a large number of the inmates of the camp spoke Sinhala fluently, and there were other intermarriages too.)

The saddest cases were of those who had lost relatives. A young woman from Trincomalee was there with her two small children, her elder brother and their cousin. Her husband had disappeared, taken away by the security forces and never seen again. A middle-aged woman, her face marked by grief, was looking for a lawyer who would help to get her son released: on the way to Colombo, he had been arrested by the security forces and detained in Welikada prison. She had already lost her husband – another disappearance.

As in the case of the refugees in Britain, some of the people in the camps had originally been living in or near Colombo and had been displaced by the 1983 riots. Some of the children in these families had spent a large proportion of their lives in refugee camps. I spoke to one such family, a middle-aged couple who looked worn and ill, and their teen-aged daughter; their son was staying with relatives. The daughter told me:

• Before 1983 we were living here, and my father was working in a garage. Then in the '83 riots the Sinhalese mob came and burned our house and destroyed the garage… That time my father was not there: I and my mother and brother were there. We saw them coming, so we ran to the house of our Sinhalese neighbours.

Did the mob come to the Sinhalese houses at all?

No – they didn't know we were there. We were hiding under the bed!

But that means they knew which houses had Tamil people living in them?

Yes, yes. We came to this same refugee camp, and stayed here for two years. Then the government gave 15,000 rupees to each family, and 84 families went to Batticaloa. For one month we were in a camp there. After that they gave us a one-room house – one room and a verandah. And my father again set up a garage there. This time, army fellows destroyed our house in Batticaloa. [That was] in August 1990. [They destroyed] a lot of people's houses… We couldn't stay there – if we had stayed there, they would have come and hacked us to death…

My friend's two brothers were killed by the army fellows, and another friend's father. One woman, the army killed her husband, and she had five small children. There are a lot of families here without a husband.

We stayed four weeks in a camp in Batticaloa – a lot of people were there! There were no meals or anything, so always we were drinking kanji (rice gruel). Sometimes even that was not there. Then a government bus brought us here.

Her mother, who was thin, haggard, coughed constantly and seemed to be feverish, described in more detail what had happened:

• The armed forces were bombing and shelling us from the air. They said they were fighting the Tigers, but of course the Tigers were nowhere to be seen, we were the ones who were getting bombed. After all, you wouldn't expect the Tigers to wait around and get killed, would you? They fire some shots or throw a bomb and then they get away, vanish – they know very well how to do that. But we, we can't get away so easily; we're sitting targets when the bombers come. And after the bombs, the Muslim Home Guards come on the ground, they break what is left of our houses and loot everything – even the roofing and other parts of the house itself. We had nothing but the clothes we were wearing when we came; even these few things here were given to us after we came.

This mode of operation was confirmed by many others: bombing and shelling from above, home guards on the ground. The purpose of the exercise was apparently to clear Tamils out of the area – although, paradoxically, some of them were there only because they had earlier been cleared out of Colombo and other parts of the South!

Who do you think is responsible for all the violence and killing?

Oh, that's the government's fault, isn't it? It's the government's duty to protect people and their lives, and they can do it too, they have the power. If they tell the army not to kill civilians, then the army will have to listen to them, the government is so powerful. They can protect people if they want to.

What about the Tigers?

The Tigers are the same; they are no better than the army. They also harass people, they also kill civilians. The problem is that neither the armed forces nor the Tigers are the least bit concerned about people. They are fighting for their own reasons, but they're not at all bothered about what happens to ordinary people. We are the ones who are suffering because neither side takes any trouble to avoid hurting us.

She also spoke of the fear of rape, especially of her young daughter, and of the time her husband had been beaten almost to death by the EPRLF, who accused him of helping the Tigers: he had been found unconscious, and had taken eight months to recover. Her husband commented bitterly on the irony of the fact that they were back in the same refugee camp after having worked so hard to rebuild their lives in Batticaloa, having lost everything they possessed for the second time, reduced to destitution once again. 'How can we live like this?' he asked. 'We are being fed, but what sort of life is it? We can't live like this!'

His voice expressed the despair and humiliation which many of these hard-working, self-reliant people must have felt at being forced to live on hand-outs, without any prospects of improvement in the foreseeable future. He wanted me to write and publish a report about the refugee camps, saying emphatically that 'People should know what we're going through.' And indeed, I found that even within Sri Lanka there was a great deal of ignorance about the sufferings of this very large section of the population who have been displaced.

A young man had left Jaffna in 1989 to avoid forcible conscription by the militants. His parents had remained in Jaffna throughout the troubles, but his father had just come to check that he was all right, since they were anxious about him. Their house was damaged by the shelling, and the neighbouring house was completely destroyed. 'Isn't your mother afraid to stay alone at home?' I asked. 'She goes to the camp when there is shelling,' he replied. The young man had been a driver in Jaffna, and wanted to know if he could find work in Colombo.

Another young man had come with his wife from Kilinochchi because he would have been forced to join the armed struggle if he had stayed. Many others were students, with no idea when or how they would be able to continue their education; they had come because they didn't want to join the

Tigers. This seemed to be the main reason why most of the young men had fled, although they were at the same time afraid of the security forces. It was impossible to avoid the conclusion that the majority of them had become refugees because *they didn't want to fight or kill anyone*. But the horrifying implication was that the security forces and Tigers, between them, gave young men in the North and East no other option but to fight or flee; to stay behind without fighting was to risk being targeted by both parties. This dual dilemma was expressed by a young man who had fled from Batticaloa when the fighting started:

Do you want to go back home when the troubles are over?

> • Now we can't go – we'll just get chopped to pieces if we go now.

Who will do that?

> The army and the Muslims [Home Guards]. The problem is that some people want to divide the country. It's impossible to divide the country! But you can't say that there – if you do, you'll get killed by the Tigers. Only here can we say such things.

Another young man who had come from Batticaloa in August 1990 to escape the fighting between the LTTE and the military had left his parents, four brothers and two sisters in camps in Batticaloa; his house had been bombed by the army in June. He was more favourable to the Tigers:

> • If the government and the LTTE have talks again, the problem could be solved… The government was saying one thing and doing another – they didn't mean what they said. The LTTE is fighting for a reason – the needs of the Tamil people are their priority.
>
> Earlier, Tamil leaders have talked, but fighting has been more effective. In the earlier talks, there were four demands: (1) self-determination, a federal state; (2) they must stop their colonisation plans; (3) language equality; and (4) security. The government must discuss these, especially self-determination for Tamils; fighting will go on until they get a separate state within a federal structure. Provincial councils fell short of a proper federal arrangement because they were not given enough rights. If they had been given enough rights, the fighting would not have started again; but why would so many lives have been lost just for the right to issue bicycle licences?! The provincial councils were like a still-born child. The government is not serious about solving the problem because they

get benefits from it, like a beggar exhibiting his sores in order to get money.

Do you have any Sinhalese or Muslim friends, colleagues or neighbours?

Yes, I have Sinhalese and Muslim friends in Batticaloa.

What will happen to them if there is a separate state?

They could stay on there.

Will they be safe?

That's a difficult question. At the moment, because of the fighting and disturbances, they are getting attacked. But after there's a separate state, they can come back if they want to.

In one of the camps, I spoke to a group of young women aged from 15 to 31; they told me their stories, and then had a discussion about the situation.

The first had come from Trincomalee in June 1990 with her parents when the army attacked them. She heard afterwards that their home had been destroyed.

The second, also from Trincomalee, came with her parents in April 1991 when the Sinhalese commandos attacked: they were coming in the night and taking away young people.

The third came from Vavuniya with her parents in June 1990 because the LTTE and army were fighting, helicopters were bombing, and they were afraid. They were living in the jungle for ten days, thirty miles from town, and got away by walking at night. They later heard that all the houses had been destroyed.

The fourth had come from Mullaitivu with her husband and parents for St Anthony's Festival in early June 1990, and couldn't go back because the fighting broke out.

The fifth came from Jaffna with her husband and five sons in October 1990 because of the bombing and disruption of her children's schooling; she was also afraid that her sons, the eldest of whom was 14, might join the Tigers. However, the eldest boy had disappeared after they came to Colombo: one day he went to the library and never came back. Her husband searched for him, going as far as Vavuniya, but failed to find him. He was not likely to have gone off on his own accord since he was a quiet boy, more like a girl, who spent most of his time alone or with his mother. Another boy with him had also disappeared. (This chilling story highlights the fact that

Colombo, and the South in general, is by no means a safe place for Tamils to be; many have been picked up and some, like these boys, have never been seen again.)

The sixth had come from Kalmunai in October 1990. She lived on the border with a Muslim village, and said that Muslim informers had denounced Tamils to the army. After the war started, about 45 people were rounded up; among them were her husband and two brothers, but she got them released after five days. Her home town was Anuradhapura, but she left in 1985 after rioting there.

The seventh had come from Vavuniya with her husband and two children in July 1990, afraid of the constant bombing; they had spent ten days in the jungle and walked nine miles. She was originally from Badulla, where her father was an estate staff worker; her husband had been a student in Kandy, but had moved to Vavuniya after the '83 riots.

The eighth had come from Vavuniya in October 1990 with her parents, four brothers and a sister, due to fear of the army. Their house had been destroyed by bombs. They were Hill-country Tamils, and she had been a domestic worker in Colombo at the time when her parents moved to Vavuniya. One of her brothers, who had been a domestic worker in Kandy from the age of five, had disappeared four months ago.

The ninth had come from Batticaloa in September 1990 with her husband and child. They had been living on the border with a Muslim village, and when the fighting broke out in June 1990, Tamils went to a refugee camp three miles away; their houses were burned by Muslim Home Guards. On September 3rd, the army came to the refugee camp, rounded up and arrested 143 inmates, including her husband's brother, who was never seen again. Following that incident, they walked through the jungle to the town, and came to Colombo after three days. Her husband's parents were still at home, but didn't want him to come back.

The tenth had come from Batticaloa with her husband in June 1990, when they had been attacked by Muslim Home Guards and the army.

The eleventh had come from Batticaloa with her husband and three sons in December 1990, after spending four months in a refugee camp in Batticaloa. Muslim Home Guards supported by the army had hacked her husband's father and brother to death and taken away her brother.

In the discussion they said, among other things:

• Only because people are armed has the problem got so bad. Otherwise it wouldn't be so bad.

• Yes, now the problem is the people with arms. But the problem started because people – especially the educated youth – didn't have employment. If everyone had food and employment, they wouldn't have started fighting.

• Since '58 the Tamils have been suffering. Our parents went from Anuradhapura to Jaffna, Jaffna to Colombo – there's no freedom anywhere, we get chased from one place to another.

• Since 1958 the old men have been talking and wasting time. Now the young men are taking up arms and wasting time!

I asked if they thought the fighting would stop if the government could supply enough jobs, food, housing and education for everyone.

• No – first the fighting must stop, then they must provide jobs and food and all those things.

• Somehow we must get freedom, even if we have to live on kanji!

The experience of repeated displacement – being chased from place to place – was a common one. Another woman, a Hill-country Tamil originally from Badulla, had moved to Colombo after marriage, and then been displaced to Batticaloa after the 1983 riots. When the ceasefire broke down in June 1990, her family fled to a refugee camp in Batticaloa, but while they were there, Muslim Home Guards came and killed her 15-year-old son. She then came to Colombo with her husband and three younger children. Her husband had gone back with six others to try and get compensation for her son, but he and four of the others had not returned. The two who did return said that the other five had been arrested by TELO [Tamil Eelam Liberation Organisation]. So she wanted money to go and try to get her husband released.

Hill-country Tamils have been among the worst sufferers, because they were attacked not only along with all other Tamil-speaking people, but also on separate occasions when they were specifically targeted. To quote one example:

When the United Front government implemented the Land Reform Law in 1972, thousands of Tamil estate workers were thrown out of the estates. They had to beg on the streets. Some died of starvation and some fled to the North Central Province. The traditional Left never raised any kind of protest against the hooliganism of the thugs. In a number of plantations, SLFP hooligans and thugs set fire to the barrack type lines of the plantation workers, stole their belongings and harassed them. (Jayaratne Maliyagoda, 'The Working Class in Recent Years', *Satyodaya*, January 1981).

Since their accommodation was tied to their jobs, these Tamils were exceptionally vulnerable because loss of employment automatically made them refugees. Thus, not only those thrown out during nationalisation of the plantations, but also others who had been sacked after a strike, had become refugees. Several families who had been victims of rioting in 1986, had lived in a refugee camp since then.

As some of the interviews quoted earlier indicate, the Hill-country Tamils resettled in the Northern and Eastern provinces were still not allowed to live in peace but continued to be subjected to periodic attack. There were some to be found in the Tamil refugee camps in Colombo, but many had taken refuge with relations who had remained in the plantation areas, sharing their over-crowded quarters and inadequate diet because they were not receiving any rations on their own account. I travelled to Nawalapitiya to interview some of these Hill-country Tamil refugees, who told me their stories.

One couple with two teenage children were born on an estate in the Kotmale area, and had gone to Batticaloa because a Muslim merchant had promised the man a tinker's job. He was earning well and living peacefully, but came back when fighting broke out in 1990 because he couldn't get work and his family was starving. Now he was living with his cousin and was still unemployed. He had worked in a workshop in Kattankudy since 1983, and his Muslim employers used to warn him not to come to work if there was trouble between Muslims and Tamils; he had plenty of Muslim friends, and felt no tension between himself and them.

Another couple with three children came originally from an estate in Ratnapura. They moved to Trincomalee in April 1983, having bought three-quarters of an acre of land there, but in July their house and all their belongings were burned; 24 houses, all belonging to Tamils, were burned in one night. They spent three months in a refugee camp, but after the birth of another child they rented a house from a Tamil in Trincomalee town. Three years later, while visiting Colombo for a relation's wedding, they heard that for the second time their home and belongings had been burned, by Sinhalese and Muslim Home Guards and security forces. So they stayed on in Colombo till 1988, then went back and rebuilt a house on the original site, using Rs 6000 which the government had given them. They were doing quite well until in June 1990 their home was burned yet again, along with several other houses; they were not sure by whom, since the people came in the night, but thought they were Sinhalese Home Guards. They took refuge in a church, and in September were evacuated to a refugee camp in Colombo by the government. From there they had come to stay with relatives in one of the plantations. In Trincomalee they had had good Sinhalese and Muslim friends.

One middle-aged woman, born in an estate near Nawalapitiya, had gone to live with her husband in Mannar after getting married in 1954, and was helping him to run a shop there. In 1988 her husband was severely assaulted by the army and died after being taken to the hospital; they were warned by the army not to say anything about the beating. She was then running the shop with her 27-year-old son, but a rival Muslim merchant denounced her son to the army, saying he was a member of the LTTE, and the security forces came and assaulted her and her son in July 1989. So she sent her son to India, and later came back to stay with her relatives on the plantation. She had a very good relationship with her Muslim neighbours, some of whom had escorted her up to Kurunegala; but she had also heard rumours that Muslim informers were giving information to the army, and was not sure if it was true.

A middle-aged man had moved from the estate to Vavuniya district in 1980 and settled there. In October 1990, people came at midnight and chased them out. They hid for three days in the jungle, and when they went back, found that their houses had been looted and stripped. So they walked to Vavuniya where the army gave them train tickets. He was now staying with his son-in-law on the estate.

In the brief discussion, the following opinions were expressed:

• If the problem is solved, I would like to go back to Mannar.

• I don't want to go back to Trincomalee! We have been affected by the violence there three times already! We don't want the country to be divided, we only want peace.

• That's right, we only want peace. Because of all this fighting, we have no place to stay, no jobs and no food.

• There has to be a political solution – fighting won't solve anything. The situation here is a bit better; there it's so bad that even the children feel hatred. So I prefer to be here.

• They're fighting, we're suffering. The government failed to solve the problem from the beginning, that's why it has got worse. I agree that peace is necessary, but now we are facing the problem of where to get our next meal!

It is worth noting, at this point, that some Muslim refugees too had fled due to indiscriminate attacks by the army in its fight against the Tigers. Muslim refugees in Colombo spoke of Muslim casualties in the security forces' bombing and shelling of Mannar city, and the fact that they had been displaced to outlying villages as a result. And I met others in a camp of about 50 families in Puttalam. They had been living on the Mannar-Puttalam Road, and had initially fled and settled further down the road when the fighting broke out in June 1990; but in August the government had shifted them to the camp in Puttalam. The Tamils from their area had already fled earlier on; they themselves escaped on foot, some people getting blown up by landmines on the way. In their own village they had been agricultural people, cultivating rice; the women used to work at home, a few doing tailoring or beedi-rolling.

The men in the camp were now mostly unemployed, but the women, after coming to the camp, had with admirable resilience and resourcefulness learned how to make winnowing fans out of palmyra leaves. They prepared the leaves collectively, and sold the winnows for fifty rupees each; they showed us a couple: they were crudely but attractively made. I asked the refugees:

If there is peace, would you like to go back?

> • Even if there is peace, we don't have any homes to go back to – our homes have been destroyed.

How do you know your homes were destroyed? Have you had any news from your village?

> No, but the army was throwing grenades at all the houses along the road, so it's very likely that ours would have been destroyed. Besides, [pointing at a derelict hut which had been abandoned], look at the state of that hut after being left for only two months! Ours have been left for 14 months, they'll be in a much worse state even if any of them have survived the grenades.

If there is peace and you are given assistance to rebuild your homes, would you want to go back?

> Yes, then we would go back.

The experiences suffered by all these Tamil-speaking refugees, within the camps and outside, were similar to the experiences which had led to the flight of the refugees in Britain. However, there were two major differences in their current situation:

(1) The degree of material deprivation and hardship suffered by the refugees in Sri Lanka was much greater; surveys indicated high levels of malnutrition (especially among children) and disease. Although many of the refugees in Britain had failed to find employment and were living on social security, they were not subjected in quite the same way to forced inactivity and the humiliation of being totally dependent, nor to the soul-destroying lack of privacy suffered by the people displaced within Sri Lanka.

(2) The refugees in Sri Lanka were still in areas where Tamils had been attacked in the past and could be attacked in the future – indeed, many of them had returned to places from which they had earlier been driven out by anti-Tamil violence, and there were occasional cases of disappearances of camp inmates. The degree of security in Britain was greater – although admittedly being undermined by politicians and tabloids who instigated attacks on refugees, and racist thugs who carried them out.

However, in both these respects, the refugees I interviewed in the South were much better off than those who had remained in the North and East. This was clear from the references some of them made to their experiences in camps in those areas. But I would also like to quote from UTHR (University Teachers for Human Rights) (Jaffna) reports to give a better picture of the nightmare existence of thousands of refugees still remaining in the Northern and Eastern Provinces.

Special Report No. 1, 25/8/90 (Jaffna):

Churches and schools have been bombed even when they functioned as refugee camps, killing a number of refugees (Preface).
The relief sent by the government in the form of food and medicines to the affected areas is far from adequate. Many refugees died of starvation and disease (Preface).
5.8.90. Two Machetti bombers attacked a refugee camp at St Anthony's Church, Passaiyoor. According to eye witnesses no militants were around, and apparently there was no provocation to attack this place. Three rocket propelled bombs were fired into the camp, one falling straight into a group of refugees who were cooking a meal. Six people were killed and thirteen were injured. Out of the six who died four were children (Preface).

On the 8th August the bomber attack on St Patrick's College refugee camp, at 8.45 am, left 3 dead and 26 injured (Preface).

Report No. 5, 10/9/90

(Eastern Report):
Pottuvil: Following the outbreak of war, all Tamils were rendered refugees, a large number of them fleeing to Thirukkovil. Towards the end of June, the STF command at Pottuvil sent a message through a senior government official that it was safe for the people to go back and that they would be protected. The people did go with hesitation and shortly after their return, the STF did a round up and took all their young men away. The people had no one to complain to. The government official who had persuaded them to go had remained behind in Thirukkovil. The young men have since not been heard of. A grieving mother said, "Oh God, why did I go back to Pottuvil? I had three sons and lost them, and am back to being a refugee" (Chapter 2).
(Jaffna Report):
A situation report sent by Fr. M.E. Pius of the Jaffna Diocesan Human Development Centre contains the following: "...The situation of the refugee camps is very pathetic. The refugee camps and their surroundings have been bombed very often... Many are dying of hunger and disease... The fortnightly government ration of food had been given only twice during the last two months and that too had not reached all the refugee camps... No water could be supplied to the refugee camps since the bowsers [water trucks] are being bombed... There are now over 327,000 persons in 396 refugee camps in the Jaffna district" (Chapter 8).
(Eastern Province, Southern Sector):
On the 20th (June), the Karaitivu refugee camp which was set up in a school and was flying a white flag, was bombed from a helicopter, killing 3 and injuring 3... A female teacher who went from the Kalmunai refugee camp to ask for food from the GS (headman) was raped by the army (Chapter 9).

Special Report No. 3, 16/10/90:

In the Amparai District... Tamils were being evicted from one place after the other... Several tens of thousands of refugees were now gathered in Thirukkovil, Thambiluvil, Kallianthivu, Sinnathottam and Vinayagapuram. On 20th September, the STF started its round ups in these areas. From the 24th dead bodies, some headless, and heads without bodies started appearing along the coast at Vinayagapuram, Thambiluvil and Thambattai. Refugees who often had no change of clothes, had inadequate shelter against the oncoming rains, were hungry and sometimes caught pneumonia, were now stricken with another source of terror. "Whom can we tell these to?", "Who will do anything at all?" are anguished cries one frequently hears. Picking up refugees for human shields during operations has also become a regular practice (Chapter 1).

In Veeramunai, the refugee camp was attacked on 12th August by Muslim hoodlums backed by the police. At Sorikalmunai, on the 18th September, following such an attack the army fired at refugees trying to flee the church (Chapter 1).

It can be safely said that well over half the Tamil population in the Eastern Province are refugees by design. Out of the 60,000 Tamils in the Amparai District, outside Thirukkovil-Thambiluvil, Kalmunai and Karaitivu, few Tamils are living in their homes. Thirukkovil-Thambiluvil has a refugee population of 10-15,000… In many communities, a high proportion of males have been slaughtered. It is about 10% or more in Veeramunai and is much higher in smaller Tamil communities in the interior parts of Amparai District. The number of widows, orphans and elderly parents who have lost their sons is significant. The men are often missing or demoralized, it is often the women who go in search of missing boys and who get about trying to find food for the families. A lady who was distributing forms for entering appeals for missing persons found that every woman was asking for not one, but a couple of forms – son, father, brother, nephew, etc… Many of the women were illiterate, and the younger ones often pregnant (Chapter 3).

On 2nd August, forces wearing a mixed bag of uniforms surrounded the refugee camp (in Pottuvil) and took away 150 males. 30 of them were later released. What remains of the rest remains unknown (Chapter 5).

Sorikalmunai… is predominantly Roman Catholic with a population of about 3000. From the beginning of hostilities in June, the villagers became refugees at Holy Cross Church… On 12th September, the army came to the church and took away 7 men… On the morning of 16th September, the army with Muslim home guards arrived in trucks, armoured vehicles and motor cycles, surrounded the church and took away 28 males. The refugees were both leaderless and thoroughly frightened. At midnight the same day, Muslim home guards arrived and forced their way into the church.

According to the people, they were backed by members of the forces… They started molesting women. Some were grabbed by their hair and were beaten against the floor. They then abducted 12 women and made their exit.

The following morning, the STF arrived to drop 3 boys from a party they had detained earlier. The boys had injuries including fractures… The people spent another night in fear.

When morning came (18th), the people decided to flee, either to Karaitivu or to Thirukkovil. One group, including old men and women stumbling along with the help of sticks, was sighted by the army at Chavalakkadai who fired two shells… some of the people retreated screaming to Sorikalmunai while others kept moving to Thirukkovil. The witnesses we spoke to included women and elderly men. The women who had been abducted included pregnant mothers. Some of them had made their way back to the church in the morning, while others with their clothes rent had been abandoned about the place. Others had to take clothes and fetch them (Chapter 5).

<u>Report No.7, 8/5/91</u>

<u>(The Refugee Camp at the Eastern University, Vantharamoolai)</u>
On 25th July, the army came to the Eastern University refugee camp about 5 pm. 10,000 refugees were in the camp at that time. The army left after taking 5 persons with the help of TELO informants…

The LTTE was… irritated by losing its civilian cover in the surrounding areas. Instead of being sympathetic to the refugees who had suffered much, it became angry with them, accusing them of eating sufficiently, having electricity and watching television, while they were in difficulties outside. Towards the end of August the transformers supplying electricity to the university were blasted. This act was an indication that the LTTE did not approve of the camp and was feeling around for means to make it uninviting…

Early morning on 5th September, the army surrounded the camp and wanted men and women to line up separately in the grounds. These inmates were then paraded before informers… Of those who were paraded, 159 were taken away. There was much anger over this. A senior member of the university staff said: "The Muslim informers brought by the army simply pointed at anyone they knew. A young boy I knew well and who was taken away, was timid and would not even have so much as spoken to the Tigers." A Christian clergyman who ministered to a number of army officers said: "The whole thing was a sham. My sister's neighbour was a fishmonger whom I know well. He had no connection with the Tigers. Someone must have been trying to get rid of a business competitor..."

The army made a similar raid on the camp on 23rd September. On this day fighting had taken place between the army and the Tigers at Kaluwankerny, a fishing village 3 miles east.

Following this, 500 people from the village came to the refugee camp. Not relishing being alone in the village the Tigers ordered the villagers to get back, threatening penalties... On 27th September the Tigers abducted the university registrar for a so-called enquiry (later released) and about the same time told the inmates of the camp that they must vacate by the 1st October... By 1st October... the home of 40,000 persons stood empty. Some of the people found their way to Batticaloa. But the larger number had headed for starvation and perils, natural and man made, in the surrounding jungles (Chapter 4).

STF Round Up of Refugee Camp, 12th December 1990

At 5.30 am the STF surrounded the refugee camp at Vipulananda College. Refugees from each village were asked to come out in turn, and were marched past persons described as Muslim informers. 28 persons were taken into custody. The manner in which persons were picked up was reminiscent of what happened in the Eastern University... Of the 28 taken, only one person from Attapalam was released. The rest are missing, mostly without any indication about their fate (Chapter 2).

Report No.8, 28/8/91

Siththandy, 21st August 1990: At 5 pm army personnel from the Morrakkaddanchenai camp took away 44 persons from the refugee camp at Sri Murugan Temple, Siththandy, who are since missing. They were mostly students, labourers and fishermen. This... suggests that the taking away of 159 persons from the refugee camp at Vantharamoolai Eastern University was one publicised instance of a practice widespread in the Batticaloa District about that time... The widespread nature of these disappearances, together with the numbers involved, point to connivance at high level...

Following the onset of the current war, the army started moving towards Batticaloa. On 20th June 1990, several bodies with cut injuries were seen on the northern outskirts of Kiran...

Many refugees then moved into Christa Seva Ashram, under the care of Sevak Sam Alfred... In August 1990 a rumour went around that the LTTE had buried mines in the surrounding area… The army then came to the Ashram refugee camp and took away about 60 persons. These persons were marched in front as mine sweepers, and the army came behind (Chapter 2).

If the fate of refugees exiled in an alien country can be described as sad, even tragic, there is only one way to describe the condition of these refugees in their own country: it is utterly intolerable. In reply to the question 'How can we live like this?' I had to agree that human beings could not possibly be expected to put up with such conditions. Yet thousands of people have lived through this daily torment for years on end; and not only people in the rest of the world but even a shamefully large number of people in Sri Lanka itself are quite oblivious of their sufferings. Surely this situation cannot go on indefinitely! It is dehumanising for everyone concerned – the refugees themselves as well as those who allow this intolerable situation to persist. It is true that there are a few courageous and dedicated people working hard to alleviate the hardships they suffer, but despite their efforts, the problem apparently gets worse and worse. Clearly something needs to be done on a much larger scale. But what?

The refugees, both in Britain and in Sri Lanka, had thoughtful and intelligent suggestions which are in urgent need of consideration by all Sri Lankans and others who are in any way concerned about the problem. But before turning to these, I would like briefly to examine two of the movements which many of the refugees felt were responsible for the problem: Sinhala and Tamil nationalism.

Chapter 5: The 'Sinhala Buddhist' State: spiritual haven, or hell on earth?

There is virtually unanimous agreement among Tamil refugees that there would have been no war if it had not been for the discrimination against, and persecution of, Tamils. In view of this, we have to examine the main cause of all the discrimination and persecution – i.e. the attempt to turn Sri Lanka into a Sinhala Buddhist state – and see what it has meant for the majority of Sri Lankans who are Sinhalese Buddhists. That the minorities have suffered from this policy is obvious; but has the majority benefited?

One obvious way in which the war has affected the Sinhalese population is by displacing some of them and turning them into refugees. I did not meet any Sinhalese refugees from the Northern Province, and was told that many of the Sinhalese who had fled to Anuradhapura from Vavuniya District had returned home when government forces regained control over the area from which they had been displaced. The refugees I met were from the East, and I visited them accompanied by a Sinhalese friend who had earlier visited Tamil camps not only in the South but also in the East.

The Sinhalese refugee camp in a village outside Colombo was a good deal less crowded than the Tamil camps: around 110 to 125 people in a hall, similar to those which housed thousands of Tamil refugees, and spacious grounds with washing-lines hung with clothes and a sheltered corner where apparently teams of refugees took it in turn to prepare the uncooked food rations that were issued by the government. In other respects, the scenario was similar, with mats spread out along the walls, a few foam-rubber mattresses hung on lines along with the clothes, and belongings stacked up near the mats. A sewing-machine and chair were in the middle of the hall, apparently for the use of refugees who might want to make or mend their own clothes.

A small group of three women, with a couple of elderly men on the edge of their group, called out to us and asked us who we were. My friend explained that she had come before, and that I wanted to ask a few questions about how they had come to be refugees.

A woman in her late thirties said that most of them had been refugees in a Buddhist temple in Batticaloa since the disturbances in 1987, till the Tigers chased them away after the breakdown of the ceasefire in June 1990. They had been taken to the airport, put on a plane and brought to Ratmalana. Did they know what had happened to their houses? The Tigers had removed everything from them, including the roofs. Another woman said she had been a teacher in a nursery school attached to the Methodist Church. In 1987 the Tigers had closed down all the Sinhala schools and the Sinhala medium in other schools, including her own. Here she was teaching in the temple near the camp, but not getting paid for it.

Others said that they had come with nothing but the clothes they were wearing; only after coming to the refugee camp had they been given mats, mattresses and clothes. I observed that in the Tamil camps there were many Tamil people from Batticaloa who had also come with nothing but the clothes they were wearing. The first woman denied that Tamil people had anything to fear or had left Batticaloa; according to her, they were all living happily there in comfort. I assured her that there were much larger numbers of refugees in the Tamil camps. My friend (who was Sinhalese) told her about the Thirukkovil camps in the Eastern Province, where tens of thousands of Tamil refugees were living in dreadful conditions and great fear, because even the security guards appointed to protect them said that on the slightest pretext, they would be ready to kill the people in their care, that even new-born babies were "Tiger cubs' and ought to be killed.

'But it's true,' said the first woman, apparently with the agreement of the others, 'they teach them to be Tigers from the time they are small.' Both of us protested. 'It's ridiculous to say that a new-born baby who knows nothing of such things can be a Tiger; that just means you are saying that all Tamils are Tigers, which is not true,' I said.

My friend added, 'Just because a few people in a community do wrong, that doesn't mean that the whole community is bad; after all, even in our community there were people who did wrong during the JVP violence, but that doesn't mean that all Sinhalese are bad.'

The old man: 'But you can't trust the Tigers, you can't believe anything they say.'

'That may be true,' I said, 'but not all Tamils are Tigers. Many Tamils have been killed by the Tigers and some of the refugees in the Tamil camps have had relatives killed by them. Many are here to get away from the Tigers as much as the security forces – they're as much afraid of the Tigers as of the security forces.' I told them about the Tamil woman married to a Sinhalese man, and asked if there were any Sinhalese married to Tamils in this camp. The first woman started off by saying, 'No, no, there are no such people here,' but then stopped and asked what I meant. I explained again. Once again, the woman flatly denied that there were any Sinhalese married to Tamils in the camp; but an elderly man, who turned out to be her brother, indicated a thin, elderly woman wandering around, and murmured something about her being a Tamil married to one of the Sinhalese men in the camp. His sister, however, said she must be a Burgher, and reiterated her opinion that Tamils had nothing to be afraid of, that they hadn't suffered, etc.

In desperation, I told her: 'I know Tamils have been suffering for a long time, since my own family was attacked in 1958 because my father is a Tamil, and we too had to leave everything and flee just as you did. The same thing happened to many other families in 1958 and 1983 – in fact there are many refugees in the Tamil camps who had fled to Batticaloa after the 1983 riots, only to be chased back again this year.'

I had hesitated to reveal my Tamil parentage for fear of stirring up even more hostility than the argument already seemed to be generating, and at first the announcement took them aback. 'Your father is Tamil?' 'Yes.' 'And your mother? Is she Sinhalese?' 'No, she's Burgher.' Then turning to my friend (as though my ethnicity affected hers!): 'And she?'
'She is Sinhalese.'

After that the first woman was quiet for a while, but the teacher was very eager to speak. She agreed that there were many Tamil people who were not like the Tigers – for example, the priest in charge of the church to which her school was attached, a very good and courageous Tamil man; after the Tigers had closed down the Sinhala stream, she had continued to teach in the English and Tamil streams.

Then you know Tamil?

> • Yes, yes, I know it well. All of us can speak Tamil except her [indicating a third woman] – she still hasn't learned to speak Tamil after all these years, I don't know why.

She explained that the reason why people felt so bitter was that they had trusted the Tigers; when the ceasefire was declared, they had really believed that the war was over and they could get back to their normal lives. Everyone had put away their arms: even the policemen were unarmed when the Tigers attacked them.

I agreed that was a very wrong thing to do, but said it was also wrong to blame all Tamils and make them suffer for the wrong-doing of a few individuals. 'No, no, there's no such feeling here,' the elderly man assured us. 'Look' – indicating the woman whom he had told us was Tamil – 'she was our neighbour and now she's living here – that's not a problem, there's nothing like that. Why don't you talk to her?'

He called her over and she came willingly, obviously curious about what was going on. But she wanted to know absolutely everything about me and my family before she would answer any of my questions. She then confided, as though it were something she didn't want to get spread around, that her parents were Tamil Brahmins of Indian origin, and that she was married to a Sinhalese. Of course all the others, who had been her neighbours in

Batticaloa, must have known this; if the elderly man knew it, his sister must surely have known it too. Yet she had denied that there were any Sinhalese married to Tamils with such vehemence that it seemed to me she actually believed what she was saying, she had somehow convinced herself that such a thing was not possible.

When the Tigers attacked Sinhalese people in 1987 and all the others moved into the refugee camp at the Buddhist temple, the Tamil woman and her husband – perhaps because she was a Hindu – had moved into a police bungalow. They had been staying there when the recent fighting broke out, and armed Tigers had come and knocked on the window at night, wanting, she said, to take her husband away. Instead, she had gone out and talked to them and apparently succeeded in persuading them to allow her and her husband to go. She herself was a teacher of English at A level, and she said that all the people around us were her neighbours in Batticaloa. 'I could easily get a job here,' she continued; 'I have already been asked more than once. But how can we go to work from this refugee camp, where we don't even have a cupboard where we can lock up our belongings?' Having lost almost everything that they possessed, she now felt very apprehensive about leaving their meagre belongings exposed to theft. 'I won't be able to concentrate on my teaching if I'm worrying about what's happening in the camp,' she said, 'You have to settle things at home before you can do your work properly!'

We asked the whole group about their plans for the future. Most of them thought the government should give them a little land and assistance to settle down and build new homes. 'What about going back to Batticaloa – don't you want to do that?' we asked.

'No, no, it's impossible to go back to Batticaloa while the Tigers are there.'

'But suppose the Tigers are driven out?' asked my friend.

'No, the Tigers will never be driven out,' said the first woman very emphatically. I got the impression that their roots in Batticaloa were not very deep.

This conversation left us both feeling quite disturbed at their refusal to acknowledge that Tamils had any grievances, and the consequent implication that they were the only sufferers. My friend commented rather angrily that they ought to be taken to see the Tamil camps in Thirukkovil – then they would be thankful for their luck in being where they were! I thought that even a visit to the Tamil camps in Colombo would help them to come to terms with the plight of the Tamils. It appeared to us that an initial attitude of goodwill towards their Tamil neighbours had partly been transformed into suspicion and hostility by anti-Tamil propaganda on the one hand, and Tiger atrocities on the other.

The ability to look more deeply into the causes of the conflict seemed to be absent – except in one case. An elderly woman in traditional-style 'cloth' [lunghi] and jacket accosted us on our way out and asked us who we were and what we were doing. We explained, and then asked her about herself. She told us she had come from Batticaloa, but was originally from Matara District; her husband had moved to Batticaloa 45 years ago in search of work, and she herself had gone there after marriage. Most of the people here, she said, were from Galle and Matara districts and had gone to Batticaloa in search of work. She said that earlier Sinhalese migrants to Batticaloa had been accepted without any trouble by the predominantly Tamil residents; there had been peace and friendship. But all that began to change around 1957–58 with the government's new policies; there had been attacks on Sinhalese settlers.

'On Sinhalese?' I asked; 'I know there were attacks on Tamils, because my own family was affected'.

'Yes,' she said, 'here they were attacking Tamils, there they were attacking Sinhalese. It was the government policies which started it all. Now everyone is suffering: we have fled, all the Tamils have fled, so many people have been killed; the whole country is being destroyed.'

'I hope you will talk to the other people in the camp and tell them all this,' I suggested. 'Some of them seem to think that Tamils haven't suffered at all, and that all Tamils are Tigers or Tiger supporters.'

'Ah,' she said, 'I can explain to you why they think like that. Some of the Tamil families have managed to escape or send their young people away, but not all of them. So the Tigers come to the Tamil families and forcibly recruit a young person from each of them. They do it by force, but even then, the whole family comes to be known as Tiger supporters. They are trapped: even though they didn't want to give their son to the Tigers, even though he was taken by force, still they become identified as "Tigers".' The picture she gave confirmed what most of the Tamil refugees had said, but her depth of understanding was unique among the Sinhalese refugees.

If we were disturbed by our conversations in this camp, a year later we were quite horrified by what we found in the Sinhalese camps in the eastern part of Anuradhapura District, close to the border with Trincomalee District. These people had been through experiences as traumatic as those suffered by the Tamil refugees: in 1990 they had been attacked by the Tigers, who had massacred large numbers of villagers, including children. Several thousands of refugees lived in these camps, which consisted of settlements of cadjan huts, and many of the families there had lost relatives.

We went with a Tamil Christian priest, who remained in his jeep, and were shown around by a Sinhalese sister from a Christian convent. At the first camp, she called a sort of meeting; most of the talking was done by the camp 'leader', a demagogic middle-aged man, and a tall, well-built young man, with occasional interjections from mostly middle-aged to elderly women. They said they were still living in considerable insecurity, since anyone who wandered too far from the camps – for example to fish in the lakes – was liable to be killed by the Tigers; earlier there had been some such incidents and the bodies had been found. Just a few days before, two young boys of 11 and 12 had wandered away like this and disappeared, and they feared the worst.

The news which had really terrified them was that the government was going to send them back to Trincomalee District in less than two weeks, and put them into camps there whether they wanted to go or not. They didn't want to go – they were convinced they would be slaughtered – but they would have no choice in the matter: their rations in this camp would be stopped and they would be taken to Trincomalee in army trucks, not to their homes, which were in various different places in the district, but to refugee camps. 'But why are they doing this?' we asked. They didn't know why, but had apparently been told that they couldn't stay on in Anuradhapura District and had to get back to their home district.

The sister confirmed this information, and added that the children were having problems with their schooling, and it would be better if they settled down in schools back in their home districts. It seemed to us, however, that this would not solve the problem of their schooling and might even make it worse, (a) because they would still be in centralised refugee camps, not in their home areas, and (b) because there was every chance that they would be driven out again by the Tigers. The rationale of sending them back into such obvious danger seemed to have much more to do with the government's colonisation policy and attempts to alter the ethnic composition of the Eastern Province by settling Sinhalese people there, even against their own will.

'Do you know what has happened to the Tamil people in your area?' we asked. Leader: 'We don't know what has happened to those animals, they must still be there. Only the Sinhalese have nowhere to go – they will be driven into the sea and that will be the end of it!'

I replied: 'No, there are many Tamil refugees, some of them from Trincomalee, in the Colombo camps. They have suffered the same kind of atrocities.' My friend added: 'Tamil refugees in the Eastern Province are suffering even more. Once when we were in Thirukkovil, we came across a large group of women and girls crying by the roadside. When we asked them why they were crying, they told us the security forces had taken away their menfolk earlier, telling the women to come and collect them; but when they went, the security forces denied all knowledge of their men and boys. Now they didn't know what to do, that's why they were crying. Over there, there are many refugee camps where all the males have been wiped out.'

Young man: 'These are all untrue stores!'

My friend: 'What do you mean, they're untrue? I saw these things with my own eyes!'

Young man (hastily): 'Well, we don't know anything about these things.'

Sister (also hastily): 'Yes, that's right, we don't get to hear anything about what is happening anywhere else.' (Could this be true, we later wondered? It seemed rather incredible.)

'Do you know when all this trouble started?' we asked.

Several people answered that it had started in 1983, when the Tigers started fighting the Sinhalese. We asked: 'Before that, was there any trouble between you and your Tamil neighbours?' 'No,' they assured us, 'before that, everything was fine; Sinhalese and Tamils and Muslims lived very happily together.'

We persisted: 'But the trouble started much earlier for the Tamils; it started because their rights have been denied and they have been attacked since 1958.'

Leader: 'The trouble in '58 was over the use of the letter "Shree" – the Tamils didn't want it, they protested, they caught Sinhalese people and branded them with the letter "Shree"!

We said: 'But it was mostly Tamil people who suffered in the 1958 riots and in many incidents since then. They have suffered for a much longer time the same kind of atrocities that you are suffering now.'

Sister: 'But that was not like this, it was not a case of people being hacked to death!'

Leader: 'Have you heard about the Kent and Dollar Farms? They were settled with Sinhalese convicts who were on the way to being released, and they were just lined up and shot!' (No mention of the fact that they were settled there only after the Hill-country Tamil refugees already settled on the farms had been brutally attacked and driven out.)

A woman: 'There was a case like that in one of our villages too – 30 people were just slaughtered.'

Sister: 'Some of our schoolchildren come from across the border, they come by van. Once the Tigers had waylaid the van and massacred almost everyone! Our own schoolchildren! It was so horrible, I couldn't even bear to look!'

We responded: 'Yes, it's true the Tigers have done terrible things, but the security forces have done exactly the same thing to innocent Tamil people – hacked them to death, burned them on tyres – and not just Tamil people either; during the JVP insurrection they killed thousands of innocent

Sinhalese people too, hacked them to death and burned them, we've seen the pictures.'

Leader (dropping his voice): 'Look lady, we know about the security forces too, don't think that we don't know about them. But we can't talk about such things here – you never know who may be listening.'

Sister (looking around): 'Yes, that's right, you don't know who may be listening.'

My friend launched into a small speech about how ethnic divisions benefited only the rich and powerful, while poor people of all communities were suffering. There were murmurs of agreement, and the sister wandered off.

We asked, 'So what is going to happen now?' They replied, 'What is going to happen? We will be taken there, that's all. We're helpless, we can't do anything about it.'

We asked, 'Do all of you want to stay here?'

They said: 'There are some people in this camp who want to go back, but the rest of us are afraid, we think we too will get killed if we go.'

'If you don't want to go, can't you stay behind?'

They answered: 'How can we stay? They say they will take us by force if necessary.'

At the next camp, we asked to speak to families individually, thinking that people might express themselves more freely in private, and we did, indeed, hear much more explicit criticism of the government. We first talked to a woman whose son, daughter-in-law and two grandchildren had been killed by the Tigers. She was a midwife who had been practising in the South, but had been transferred to the East because of a shortage of midwives there; she had been offered some kind of gratuity, but instead had asked for some land, and had built a house there. She said there had been trouble in her area since 1980; in 1985 the Tigers had come and gunned down 30 people, and on the 31st December 1987 her house had been burned with all her belongings, embodying savings since she started working in 1948, but there had been no compensation from the government. Even in this camp, she said, it was not the government but only the sisters who cared for them and got them what they needed.

She showed us photographs of her grandchildren, taken after they had been hacked to death; they had been given to her by the army, and my friend said she should throw them away because they would only serve to stir up hatred. However, it seemed to me she was suffering more from grief than from hatred. 'I know we all have to die some time,' she said, 'but not like this, not like this! And now I have to carry this grief and pain with me until I die. Maybe that will happen soon enough, since we are being sent back there.'

Her young daughter-in-law, who was suckling a baby, joined in vigorously at that point: 'Yes, that's what will happen, and everybody knows it; whoever survived last time will get killed this time – we're being sent to our deaths. They say the army will protect us, but we know very well what that means. Maybe during the daytime they will be around, but at night they will disappear, and that's when the Tigers will come. We'll end up hiding in the jungles as we were doing before. And how can we hide, with all these little children? You know what they're like – they cry, they laugh, they cough – it's just impossible to keep them quiet. We'll be finished off, every single one of us, that's what's going to happen.'

'But if *you* know what the situation is, and *they* know what the situation is, why are they sending you back?' we asked. 'It would be different if the war were over and there was peace, then there would be some sense in it. But what sense does it make to send you back while the war is still raging?'

'They want us to help to fight the war, that's what they say.'

'Don't any of you want to go?'

'No one from this camp wants to go.'

'Can't you stay, then?'

'They'll cut off our rations and leave us to starve. What can we do? We'll die if we go and we'll die if we stay. We heard that the AGA has been told he will lose his job unless he gets rid of us. We don't know if it's true, but that's what we've been told.'

We asked what had happened to the Tamil people in their area. The young woman told us that the Tigers had rounded them up and taken them all away, apart from two people whom they had killed, and they hadn't been seen since then.

We talked to another group of people, mostly women and girls with one young man. A middle-aged woman from Trincomalee said, 'It would be different if we were being sent to our homes – at least that would be something. But no, we're being sent to other camps which are not even near our homes.'

'When did all this trouble start?' we asked.

'In 1983,' they told us.

'Before that, was there any trouble between you and your Tamil neighbours?'

'Not at all. We lived together very happily, like brothers and sisters.'

'Do you know what has happened to them now?'

'No, we don't. The Tigers came and took them away – only two old people who couldn't walk they shot. They rounded up everyone else, including women and children, and took them away, we don't know where. We've been told they have underground camps where they keep all these people, and where they also have factories and everything else.'

They agreed with my friend that poor people of all communities, including Tamils, were suffering. Their attitude to their Tamil neighbours was a mixture of sympathy based on their previous friendship, and suspicion because they half believed the rumours that they had all gone over to the Tigers.

'What do you think is the solution to the problem of this conflict?' we asked.

'The solution? The only solution is for all of us to get killed, and that's what is going to happen,' said the young man bitterly.

'It's difficult for us to think of anything now except this problem of being sent back,' said one of the women. 'It's like dying a daily death. How can we think of anything else?'

'We have no way out. If we go, we'll be killed. If we try to stay, we won't get our rations – and in any case they have threatened they will take us by force.'

As they went on talking, they conveyed a feeling of utter fatalism and hopelessness, of being used as pawns in a game they couldn't understand, of being crushed between forces they couldn't control.

'How can this happen?' we asked the sister on the way back to the jeep. 'Surely there must be some way in which this forced deportation can be averted?'

'But you must see the standpoint of the army,' she replied. 'They are strangers to the place, they say they need local people to guide them and help them. Besides, they say, what is the point of being sent there to protect the Sinhalese residents if there are no Sinhalese residents to protect?'

We thought, but didn't say, what is the need to send in the army to protect the Sinhalese residents in the first place, if there are no Sinhalese residents there to protect? Why not simply recall the army, and get them to protect these refugees where they are? No sane person could have been taken in by this upside-down reasoning. It was obvious that these unfortunate people were being sent back to Trincomalee district for reasons which had nothing whatsoever to do with their protection or welfare, that they were being used against their will in the government's strategy to alter the ethnic character of the East, and that the sister approved of all this.

The anti-Tamil feeling not only in the refugee camps but – even more – among the sisters in the convent, made me uneasy; I began to understand why the priest who had brought us, much more obviously Tamil than I was, and isolated in Anuradhapura district from where most Tamils had been driven out by repeated pogroms, had chosen to remain in the jeep. When we had dropped the sister back at the convent, I suggested that he should try to explain to these people, at least to the sisters, about the denial of Tamil rights.

'There's no point,' he said bitterly, 'these people will never understand; they will only think I'm a Tiger supporter for saying such things. I'm no supporter of the Tigers; but as for the Tamil people, I've seen how they have suffered, and I feel very deeply about it. But I can't talk to any of these people about that. Now you've seen the situation for yourselves, you can understand how it is. It was even worse before: right in front of me they would say that all Tamils should be killed, and things like that. When the Sinhalese refugees first came, I worked night and day getting relief supplies to them, but after some months I stopped. I thought, there's no point, no point doing this without enlightening their minds; this won't solve the problem – it will just go on and on.'

My friend and I were both quite shaken by this whole experience: firstly, by the impending fate of the refugees we had met, some of whom would almost certainly be killed within a month. Surely it was their fundamental right to stay where they were if they wanted to, to refuse to be recruited – down to the last old person and tiny child – to fight a war against their will? Or did Sinhalese Buddhists have no fundamental rights in this 'Sinhala Buddhist' state?

Secondly, we were horrified by the way in which their ignorance of the fate of their Tamil neighbours and of the history of the conflict was being manipulated to generate distrust and hostility against all Tamils, bearing out the allegation by some Tamil refugees that ordinary Sinhalese people were having their minds poisoned by anti-Tamil propaganda. We knew, from friends working in Moneragala District with Sinhalese villagers who had suffered similar atrocities at the hands of the Tigers, that even in such tragic circumstances it was possible to promote understanding between the two communities; indeed, my friend, in the short time she had at her disposal, was already able to make an impact.

We had thought that the sisters, with their superior access to information and religious commitment to being peace-makers, would be playing such a role. But they seemed, on the contrary, to be promoting the notion of collective punishment among the refugees they served: the irrational blaming of all Tamils for the atrocities of a few, the callous disregard of the sufferings of the Tamil community, and the justification of atrocities committed against innocent members of it. We had heard that some Buddhist priests were promoting such attitudes, but had not known that Sinhalese Christians were doing the same. We sympathised with the Tamil priest's feeling that it was pointless doling out relief and rehabilitation to the refugees so long as the relief supplies were contaminated with the poison of communal hatred.

Interestingly, his sentiments were echoed and amplified by a Sinhalese refugee in the camp near Colombo. 'Look at all these people here,' she said, indicating the other refugees. 'They are asking for a plot of land and assistance to build a house over here. But supposing they get what they want... Will that solve the problem? No. Because they will always feel: it was because of those Tamils that we were driven out of our homes. So the hostility and resentment will remain. And the same with Tamil refugees. Even if they are given a piece of land and a house somewhere, they will still feel, it was because of those Sinhalese or Muslims or whatever that we were driven out of our homes. And they too will feel hatred and hostility. Hatred will lead to violence, and violence will lead to more violence, and so it will go on until the whole country is destroyed. So is that the solution? No, it's not. What is the solution? The only solution is to have friendship between communities as we used to have earlier. Isn't that the only solution? How else can we solve our problems?'

We had to agree with her. Promoting friendship between communities as a way of breaking the vicious circle of hatred and violence: that made sense to us. But friendship is possible only between equals, and the past she was referring to was the time before attempts to create a Sinhalese state had converted members of minority communities into second- or third-class citizens. 'Have you noticed that it is always the poor who suffer?' she asked. 'The rich people somehow manage to escape and get away, they don't have to suffer the consequences of all the devastation. It is the poor people of all communities who have lost everything they had. Look at us now, completely destitute, no better than beggars. And yet, after all, we are the lucky ones: we have escaped with our lives and limbs. With a bit of help, we can manage to survive. But what about those who have lost their arms and legs? Who is going to give them back their limbs? And what about those who have been killed? Who is going to bring them back to life? Tell me, who is going to bring them back to life?'

A simple woman in cloth and jacket, she was speaking in private to the two of us. But I feel her words should be put to every Sinhalese person in Sri Lanka, because what she is suggesting is of the utmost importance: she is pointing out that the conversion of Sri Lanka into a 'Sinhala Buddhist' state has not benefited poor people in the majority community, but has, on the contrary, made life much harder for them; it is her contention that most Sinhalese people – since the rich are only a minority – have suffered as a result of the government's policies.

Is she right? This is a question that the Sinhalese people in Sri Lanka can answer better than I can. But the scattered evidence I came across tended to support her view. According to records compiled by SEDEC [Social and Development Education Centre], on 30th August 1990 there were 934,501 displaced persons in 694 camps throughout Sri Lanka. In August 1991, according to Mr P. Dayaratne, Minister of Rehabilitation, Reconstruction and Social Welfare, there were 1,640,000 refugees in the country (*The Island*, 24/8/91, 'Minister Dayaratne and officials discuss refugee problem'). This is a massive number of displaced people, approximately one-tenth of the island's population; according to Mr Dayaratne, it cost nearly Rs 150 million a month to provide them even with the inadequate rations they were receiving – a severe drain on the economy, to which must be added the loss in production caused by their displacement.

Already by November 1987, when the situation was not yet so bad, a World Bank report was saying:

> The conflict has disrupted activities in all sectors of the economy – farming, fishing, manufacturing, transport, trade – put a heavy burden on both the budget and the balance of payments, and caused damage to the country's infrastructure estimated to be at about US$700 million. This US$700 million is only a portion of the quantifiable economic losses that the country has suffered. The decline in tourist arrivals after the beginning of the conflict caused US$200 million reduction in foreign exchange earnings since August 1983. Another US$500 million had to be allocated to strengthen the security forces, some US$300 million of which was for imports of military equipment. About US$250 million of foreign investment that could have materialised in the last four years under normal conditions were lost because foreign investors were reluctant to invest in a country with an uncertain political climate. Lost agricultural and fishing production is estimated to be at US$250 million. All in all, the ethnic conflict has caused since its beginning losses to the economy that are probably over US$2 billion…
>
> Almost 100,000 families, of which about 90,000 were farmers and fishermen, lost their homes; with an average of 5 people per family, that translates to 500,000 people homeless…
>
> The northern and eastern parts of the country suffered the greatest disruption… Many workplaces were destroyed or damaged, and thousands of others closed… Thousands of farmers were forced to leave their lands and in some areas, the irrigation systems they are so dependent on were damaged… whole fishing villages were destroyed… Schools were damaged and others forced to close… Similarly, some hospitals and clinics were damaged… (Sri Lanka Reconstruction and Rehabilitation Program, World Bank Report No. 6998-CE, 6/11/ 87).

And so it goes on, detailing the destruction of housing, commercial businesses, agriculture and fisheries, irrigation, water supply and sanitation, roads and bridges, public transport, railways, telecommunications, power, industry, education, health services and public buildings. By 1990-91, the number of homeless people had more than trebled, the destruction had continued unabated, and the Ministry of Rehabilitation estimated that the losses to the economy had doubled. To this must be added the heavy cost of the continuing military build-up. The main direct sufferers from the ethnic conflict might have been Tamils, but the devastation of the economy affected Sinhalese too, leading to increased poverty and unemployment.

During my second visit in 1991, a UNP MP was reported in the newspapers as complaining that when Sinhalese youth in his constituency asked for employment, the only avenue open to them was the security forces – which, of course, is not a particularly safe or healthy occupation in a time of war. I have no figures of Sinhalese soldiers dead or injured during the course of the war, but casualties were reported to be high when the fighting was heavy, and many thousands of Sinhalese young men must have been killed or maimed – in addition, that is, to the civilians attacked by the Tigers.

While standards of living deteriorated for the majority of Sinhalese people, there is also a great deal of evidence that the democratic and human rights of ordinary Sinhalese people were being eroded at the same time. Sri Lanka, once renowned for the conduct of free and fair elections, completely lost this reputation from 1982 onwards, when electoral fraud and intimidation were reported on an alarming scale (Samarakoon 1988, p. 19; Senewiratne 1986). Most horrifying of all were the well-documented reports of attacks on Sinhalese civilians by the security forces and state-backed vigilante groups during the counter-insurgency operations against the JVP (see Amnesty International reports).

The very fact that the JVP insurrection took place indicates that a significant section of the Sinhalese population was dissatisfied with the government which ruled in their name. However, it cannot therefore be assumed that all Sinhalese people in the areas where the JVP was active supported it, or approved of its extremely violent methods; and the violent methods of the JVP are certainly no justification for the way in which thousands of Sinhalese youths were tortured and executed without trial, their bodies hacked to pieces and dumped in rivers or left burning by the roadside. During my first visit, people were still stunned by the murder of Richard de Zoysa, a well-known journalist and critic of the government, and the death-threats against his mother and her lawyer, who were trying to pursue the case against the police officers they accused of murdering him. It was widely felt that if someone as well-placed as de Zoysa could be so easily killed and his killers go scot-free, ordinary Sinhalese youth must be even more vulnerable. And indeed, the Mothers' Front, which his mother helped to found, documented the disappearance of tens of thousands of Sinhalese youths during the counter-insurgency operations. The case of a Sinhalese lawyer tortured to death by the security forces also received wide publicity. (See Amnesty International reports for both these cases.)

Talking to people from a couple of hill-country villages, I got some sense of the nightmare endured by ordinary Sinhalese people trapped between the violence of the JVP and that of the security forces. A man from a JVP stronghold around eight miles from Kandy said that the JVP was supported mainly by young men of 18 to 30 years old, but also by some young women and schoolchildren of 14 to 18; most of them were educated up to O level, and unemployed. Their families owned very little land and got no income from it; most of them had parents who worked as carpenters, masons and so forth on a casual basis. The period of maximum activity was 1987 to 1989, but the violence had escalated in September 1989 when the JVP put up posters saying that unless all army personnel resigned, their families would be killed. In fact, one family which had two sons in the army was attacked; the father was killed and the mother and sister were cut and wounded, but survived and left the village. Another couple was killed – it was said that the wife was a strong supporter of the UNP and very critical of the JVP.

The next day around noon, army personnel, fully armed, entered the village in truckloads and set about smashing and burning houses and attacking people. They then went away, but came back in the night and killed whole families – for example, a father and three sons, a mother and father and son, etc; they brought dead bodies from elsewhere and dumped them in empty houses. Those villagers who could escape, hid in the jungle that night, and many left the place, so that it was like a ghost village. Later the police came again at night and took away people, some of whom were still missing. After about five months people started coming back, but JVP killings of suspected informers still went on. Recently, a woman who had lost her husband and three sons in the violence had been heard to say, 'They should have killed me too – it would have been a meritorious deed!'

In another village close to Nawalapitiya, I met women whose husbands had been killed, some by the JVP and some by the security forces. The first woman told us that in 1989, about three people from the village and ten from the area, including the former MP, were killed by the JVP, after which repression was let loose. 25 to 30 people were taken away. Of her husband's five brothers who were taken away, two were sent back and the rest disappeared. But her husband was taken and killed only the following year. She had kept telling him not to get involved with the JVP even if his brothers were involved, persuading him to stay at home, and she was in fact convinced that he had kept clear of them; she thought he had been taken away because he had been denounced to the police by a rival claimant in a land dispute.

She felt that the JVP violence would never have arisen if there had been sufficient jobs, food and housing to go round. Previously things had been much better for them; now the cost of living was higher and real incomes lower. At one time they could manage for a whole month with 10 rupees, but now not even 1,000 rupees was enough; the situation deteriorated dramatically when the food stamp system was introduced in 1979 and prices shot up by several hundred per cent.

Another woman's husband had been arrested on the road at night in August 1989, and had disappeared; she didn't know whether he was alive or dead. His two brothers had also disappeared. She said that about seven people had been taken by a vigilante group calling themselves 'Gonusso' ('Scorpions'), and the rest by the security forces; they had done nothing wrong, it was because there was no unity, people were divided and so they denounced each other on the basis of personal grudges.

The third woman's husband had been killed by the JVP. He had been a plantation supervisor and then a security guard; he supported the UNP, worked for the government and was known to be corrupt, taking bribes and giving jobs not to qualified youths but to those who gave him money. She and her three sons had been at home that night in July 1989 when a crowd came to their door dressed in black with black hoods. Three of them came in and started assaulting her husband; when she and the children tried to intervene, they were threatened too. The hooded gang then dragged her husband out on to the doorstep, shut the door, and proceeded to hack him to death there and then. She and the children could hear everything, and when they finally came out his corpse was there, the neck almost completely severed. After that they couldn't stay in the house, so they went to her mother's place; but they couldn't stay there for ever either, so they came back after a year, and she used the compensation money provided by the government to break down the part of the house where her husband was killed, and rebuild and improve it.

She was better off than the widows of those who had been killed by the security forces, because she had received compensation and they had not; but the money couldn't solve the problems of her children, all of whom had been severely disturbed from that day. The eldest, who was nearly 16, suffered from severe headaches, couldn't concentrate on his studies at all, and had become very withdrawn and anti-social, refusing to mix with his friends or take part in anything. The second, 14, would never stay at home, but slept at his grandmother's place and studied in his friend's house. The youngest, 12 years old, had become completely unmanageable and fought with everyone. 'The problems in our country have occurred because people don't think that other people are like themselves, that they have the same needs and the same feelings regardless of differences in race, caste or religion,' she said. 'A change has to take place in people's minds, in their thinking. So many people are armed now; but the problem can't be solved by arms, only by discussion. Now the fighting is less in these areas, but it is going on in other areas. There too innocent people are being killed. We know what they must be suffering, because we too have suffered.'

It was clear to us that the JVP, or people acting in its name, had committed atrocities; but it was equally clear that there had been no semblance of a legal procedure to establish the guilt of those who had been killed in reprisal. Another informant told us that in his village, under cover of the counter-insurgency operations, there had been an attempt to wipe out all members of the SLFP (Sri Lanka Freedom Party, which was the parliamentary opposition at the time), himself among them. He was stunned one day to be warned by a police officer who knew him that his name was third on a list of JVP suspects to be eliminated. Going to see for himself, he found it was true: the UNP MP of the area had drawn up a list, identifying all SLFP members and supporters as JVP suspects! In this case the police had refused to take action against them, but in other cases many SLFP supporters had been killed. Evidently, human rights violations by the Sinhalese state were not confined to ethnic minorities; these poverty-stricken Sinhalese villagers had gained nothing and lost a great deal – in terms of living standards as well as human and democratic rights – from the government policies carried out in their name.

This informant also confirmed my impression that their own experience of state repression had changed these people's perception of the ethnic conflict; many of them were now sceptical about the role of the security forces in the North and East, and thought they might be killing innocent people there just as they had done here, where Sinhalese were killing Sinhalese. Anti-Tamil feeling was much less now, he said; even the virulence of the Buddhist priests had abated. Recently, when the bodies of two young Sinhalese soldiers killed in the fighting were brought home, it was two Tamil boys who put up the decorations for the funeral.

I feel that all Sinhalese people in Sri Lanka need to think very seriously about the refugee woman's suggestion that the solution to their problems lies in a democratic country with equal rights for all and friendship between communities rather than a 'Sinhala Buddhist' nation where no one's rights are respected and civil war has become chronic. I put 'Sinhala Buddhist' in quotation marks because I know that many Sinhalese Buddhists feel that the whole notion of 'Sinhala Buddhism' is nonsensical, since Buddhism cannot be defined by reference to any nation or ethnic group; indeed, one Tamil informant told me that there are three major Buddhist epics written in Tamil.

Although many Tamil refugees referred to the communal role played by some Buddhist priests, there are others who have deplored the violence and have helped Tamils. A monk interviewed by Dharmasiri Bandaranayake in his film *Echoes of War* said, 'Being a refugee is a wretched condition for anybody – Sinhala, Tamil or Muslim. If you go into a refugee camp you will understand this clearly. A human being has certain essential human rights but in a refugee camp he loses all these… No human being should become a refugee.' Another spoke of sheltering Tamil refugees in the temple (see *Lanka Guardian*, 1.4.88). Indeed, many Tamils (perhaps including my own family) owe their lives to the Buddhist traditions of non-violence and compassion, and these would certainly be a resource in rebuilding a peaceful Sri Lanka.

I feel that the majority of Sinhalese people, if all the facts are laid before them and a referendum is held to decide the question, would vote for equal rights and peace rather than 'Sinhala Buddhism' and war. Because it is a mistake to think that only ethnic minorities have suffered from the attempts by successive governments to convert Sri Lanka into an exclusively 'Sinhala Buddhist' nation. The majority community has suffered too – so much so that most of them look back to the period before the ethnic conflict as a kind of golden age or paradise lost. But what has been lost can also be regained by reversing the process that led to the war; it won't be easy, but it can be done.

Chapter 6: Tamil Eelam: the only solution, or part of the problem?

There were some Tamil refugees – not many, but a few – who felt that the only solution to the problem of decades of discrimination against and persecution of Tamils was the creation of a separate Tamil state:

Are there any prospects for a positive change in the future?

> • If there is a separate homeland. Before the British came, we were separate, and we were united only because of their regime. So it's better for us to live separately… Most Sinhalese don't like the idea of a separate state, but at the same time they won't give any equal opportunities or rights to the Tamils either.

You think most Sinhalese people are like that?

> Yes. The government last year promised to give some devolution of power, but it is in writing only – in practice they don't give it… they won't ever give equal opportunities.

So you think the only solution is to have a separate Tamil state?

> Yes. Then we can be good neighbours. Otherwise Sinhalese and Tamils will always be fighting. But we can be friendly neighbours if we have a separate state.

> • First the Indian army must leave the country, and the Tamils must get a separate state… On the whole the civilians – the ordinary Sinhalese – are very good people. But the government policies have changed the country.

> • If there is a peaceful solution, Sinhalese and Tamils can live alongside each other peacefully.

Do you think the majority of ordinary Sinhalese people feel hostile to Tamils?

> No… But the Tamils can live peacefully only if they get a separate state.

Does that mean you think they can't live peacefully in a united Sri Lanka?

No, I don't think they can. However the Sinhalese got that anti-Tamil feeling, it will cause problems.

• If they can get [a separate state], that's really good. But I don't think you should get violent, using weapons and all that kind of thing.

Have you had any Sinhalese friends, colleagues or neighbours?

Not in Jaffna, but after coming to Colombo, yes. One of my uncles is married to a Sinhalese, and my grandma has a Sinhalese friend who was staying with us. We get on quite all right with Sinhalese people… They were quite helpful in Sri Lanka – you know, for getting into the government pension office or whatever, you need Sinhalese people's influence. Sinhalese people in various departments have helped us – that sort of help.

But you don't think it's possible for Sinhalese and Tamils to live alongside each other peacefully?

I would like to. I think most people want to, but they can't.

• If the government decides to agree to separation, it will be okay; otherwise the fighting will continue – they're going to fight. If there is a separate state, we can be happy – I think so… Sinhalese people are okay, but the government has created the problem, and now some of them are also against the Tamils. But some of them understand that the government has made this problem, they accept that the government has to solve this problem.

Do you think it's possible for Sinhalese and Tamils to live alongside each other?

Not now… not in the future. No. The government made this situation, and now we can't change it.

• The only solution is an independent Tamil state. Not autonomy but self-determination – a separate state. Because we have a history, and we have lost our property, our people, our culture – so far, we have lost everything. Now we have nothing to lose. So that's the only solution. The only solution is for the Sinhalese and India to give and accept independence, so that we can live together. Otherwise we can't. They must accept it, and give us an assurance that we can live with each other. They must first accept us as an independent state, and then we can decide whether we can join together in any way. Tamil Eelam and Sri Lanka and India – three states – that must be how we decide in future. If you don't accept this, and you ask us to live in one country with autonomy, that is not good enough. Because if you don't accept our independence, that means you are not willing to give anything…

We always like to live with each other – but not in one country. You see, now in Europe there is the EEC; they don't have to give up their independence when they join, only in some aspects they join and participate.

• I think the only solution is if India will accept, and the Sri Lankan government will accept, Tamils' self-determination… First [the Sinhalese] must accept our independent state: self-determination. I think the ball is in their court now.

• If the Indian army leaves, and there's a separate state, it'll be okay – the situation will improve.

Is it possible for Sinhalese and Tamil people to live alongside each other peacefully?

I don't think so, now – maybe earlier it was possible. Because ever since the problem started, it has become worse and worse.

A few felt that the time had not yet come to give up the quest for other solutions, but saw separation as a last resort if all else failed:

• I think the first thing is that the Indian troops should leave. Then the Sinhalese masses must be made to understand that the Tamils are actually part of the country, and they have their own homeland.

That Sri Lanka is your homeland?

Yes, especially the North and East, which are the traditional homelands. And they must be equally treated – not given privileges. Failing which, it's better to put up a separate state – they will be compelled to do that, there's no alternative except setting up a separate state where Tamils can live with dignity.

• If the discrimination persists and there is no other way, then we have to fight for separation. But if a government is formed with some socialist ideas, and if they're ready to give equal rights without discrimination, there's no point going away from the mainstream.

In any case, separation won't help Tamils in other parts of the country.

That's right – we have to think of those people also. I don't say that separatism is the only way; but if there's no other way – if the majority people in Sri Lanka, the Sinhalese people, are really adamant, and there's no other way – we have to separate. But I don't like that! It would be better to have a unified state with equal rights.

Vacillation between cynicism and hope sometimes resulted in ambiguity:

What about Tamils whose homes are in predominantly Sinhalese areas?

• I always thought that the separation of Eelam was something like this: like if I want, say, £100 from somebody, I would have always gone for £200… It was a way of bargaining, that's the way it started. But I don't think there's any Tamil in Sri Lanka now who wishes to remain in the South. Should there be a separate Tamil state, I don't think anybody in their sensible mind would remain.

Have you had any Sinhalese friends, colleagues or neighbours?

Yes, in Sri Lanka and Britain too. Most of my friends in school were Sinhalese… They helped my family by hiding our valuables, and keeping all the ladies in their house. That was in Colombo. But things have been different out of Colombo for my relatives… in fact, their neighbours have attacked my relatives.

Would you think it possible at some future date to live alongside one another in a unified Sri Lanka?

It could be a bit tough there, I would have thought, but hopefully yes. It could be a bit difficult, because our views have gone a bit extreme now, haven't they? I mean either way – even my Sinhalese friends would think differently now from what they would have thought before.

One Tamil woman in a refugee camp saw separation not as a solution to the problem of discrimination and persecution, but as the only way of getting the militants to stop fighting:

> • If the country isn't divided, they will go on fighting; so it may be better to divide it!

But most of the Tamil refugees did not see a separate Tamil state as any part of the solution to their problems, and some were frankly critical of the whole idea:

> • Whether you are in a separate state, or whether it is a unitary state, we have to live together. So this business of 'We will be separate' is utter rubbish! Are they going to put up a palmyra fence from Mannar to Batticaloa? And have pop guns to fight each other? These Tamil nationalists are lunatics! Utter lunatics! And hypocrites – utter hypocrites!

Has there been a confusion between the idea of self-determination with minority rights, and the idea of state power?

> Not confusion – they're not confused. What they want is power!

Another refugee added, even more ominously,

> • When Eelam comes, Tamils will kill Tamils, and more destruction will occur.

One can sympathise whole-heartedly with the desire for a homeland in which Tamils can live in peace and dignity. The question, however, is whether this can be achieved by setting up an exclusively Tamil state in the North and East. To begin with, this is no help to the many Tamils suffering persecution in the rest of Sri Lanka; those Tamils who refer to the North and East as the 'traditional homeland' of the Tamils seem to forget that this was a term used by racists in South Africa and Israel in order to keep the indigenous people out of the greater part of their own country.

In Sri Lanka, it likewise has reactionary connotations, implying, as it does, that the whole of Sri Lanka is not the rightful homeland of the Tamil-speaking people of the island, which it historically has been. It is striking how many Tamil refugees in Britain referred longingly to the whole of Sri Lanka as 'my country,' 'my own country,' 'our country,' 'our own country,' 'our home,' 'our motherland,' etc. (see Chapter 3).

But even for Tamils in the North and East, is Eelam a solution to their problems? I believe the whole concept suffers from a fundamental flaw which has led to the radical degeneration of the separatist struggle. What are the implications of defining it as a *Tamil* state rather than simply a democratic state in which people of all communities and ethnic groups have equal rights and equal status? One consequence of this ethnic nationalism was evident in the last chapter: massacres of Sinhalese civilians, including little children, have been an ugly feature of the attempt to realise Tamil Eelam. The kind of thinking which can justify such atrocities is exactly the same as the thinking which justifies killing Tamil babies on the grounds that they are Tiger cubs.

But the drive for ethnic purity in the territory claimed as Tamil Eelam has gone even further: it has been turned against the Tamil-speaking Muslim community. With the breakdown of the ceasefire in June 1990, Muslim civilians in the North and East came under attack. Prior to my visit in 1990, there were reports that on 3rd August the Tigers had massacred over 100 Muslims in two mosques in Kattankudy, and on 13th August they had carried out massacres in three Muslim villages in Eravur (see UTHR (Jaffna) Report No. 5, Chapter 2).

Then, during my visit, in one of the most bizarre episodes of the entire war, the Tigers ordered all Muslims out of the Northern Province, threatening that they would be killed if they didn't leave. They fled in panic, leaving most of their possessions. I visited some of the camps in Puttalam District, where tens of thousands of them had taken refuge. They were living in settlements of bamboo and mud huts with cadjan roofs; in some camps, two or three families in a hut, in others, a hut per family. Shortage of lavatories seemed to be the biggest problem, lack of water the next, and poor nutrition the third. Everywhere we went, the children were cheerful and extremely friendly, but some looked undernourished and/or badly dressed; most of the younger ones had been placed in local schools.

In the first camp, we spoke to a group of men and women, all middle-aged to elderly. Some of the women – around 40 of them, mostly one from each family but in some cases more than one – went out to work as labourers in onion and paddy cultivation; a few of the men were also employed in cultivation. Most of the families had been fisher-people in Mannar; the women had previously not gone out to work, but some used to make mats, baskets, and so forth, out of ola leaves. There were also five families from Mullaitivu, two tailoring and the rest labourers. They said many Muslims had left Mullaitivu in 1987 due to harassment by the IPKF; they returned in January 1990, but had been driven out again by the fighting in July. The Sinhalese people who had been living there previously had left in 1984.

The refugees from Mannar said they had no problem with the local Tamils but had lived happily together like brothers and sisters; those from Mullaitivu said that originally Sinhalese, Tamils and Muslims had all lived together happily. They felt it was the Tigers who were the problem, not the Tamils; they were afraid of being killed by the Tigers if they went back, but if not for the Tigers, would have liked to return. A few had, in fact, gone back, only to find their homes destroyed and belongings looted. They felt the problem had arisen because the Tigers wanted a separate state which was purely Tamil.

The inmates at the next camp wanted to engage in agricultural production but were unable to do so because they didn't have the means to lease land from the local owners. In a third camp, however, they had been able to acquire land, and were growing onions and other crops quite successfully. In another camp there were 100 families, all from a colony in Moor Street, Jaffna, who had come in October 1990. Most of the talking was done by a middle-aged man, leader of the camp; a middle-aged woman also put in a word from time to time. They told us most of the men had been petty traders in Jaffna and were unemployed here, although they managed the camp kadé (tiny shop) in rotation. The women had only worked at home in Jaffna, but a few went out to work here. They had never expected anything like this to happen, they said; up to that time, they had lived quite happily alongside their Tamil neighbours.

What about the future?

• The future is in God's hands!

Would you like to go back?

We're afraid we'll be killed if we do.

But if there is peace and your security is assured?

Then we would like to go back.

Have you any idea why the Tigers did this to you?

They say it's because of what the Muslims did to their people in the Eastern Province.

How did you manage to get away?

We walked for about forty miles, partly through the jungle. Then army vehicles helped to bring us here.

The Muslim camps in and near Colombo were very similar to the Tamil camps. In one, I spoke to a group of young women; one of them had come from Mannar, but the rest were all from Jaffna. They said the Tigers had called a meeting in a school on October 31, 1990, and told them to leave in two hours, taking only their clothes; apparently the Tigers had said, 'Muslims are killing Tamils in Batticaloa, but we're not killing you, we're only asking you to leave in two hours,' and had arranged a lorry to take the refugees to Colombo.

The Muslims were stunned; they had never had any problems with local Tamils, so this was like a bolt from the blue. These girls had been going to Muslim schools, but their brothers had gone to mixed schools and there were no problems; they had never felt any discrimination against them. They felt very sad to leave, but were afraid that the Tigers would kill them if they went back; even if the war ended, they would still be afraid, so they would prefer to settle in Colombo if possible. However, their fathers, most of whom were tailors, preferred to go back because their occupation was there and they could earn a better income.

Why do you think the problem started?

    • They say it's because of Muslims attacking Tamils in Batticaloa.

But Muslim Home Guards in Batticaloa have nothing to do with peaceful Muslim civilians in Jaffna or Mannar!

That's true. I think the real reason is that the Tigers are fighting for a separate Eelam. But even then, they had no reason to attack us. Although Muslims were not asking for a separate state, we didn't oppose them either. We never helped the security forces! At first the Tigers took money only from rich people, not from the poor; but now they're robbing everyone! We're praying every day that the problem will be over, so that we can at least go back and see our homes.

How do you think the problem can be ended?

We can't say. There were talks earlier, but they broke down and there was war again. Now we feel that even if there are talks, the

143

same thing could happen again! The bombs are falling there, not here, but still our minds are not at peace.

Their mothers, whom I met subsequently, were much more explicit in their agitation and outrage at what had happened. Their account of the events was similar: some Tigers had come from Batticaloa saying that Muslims were massacring Tamils there, and they should retaliate by killing Muslims in Jaffna, but the local Tigers refused to do that. Then the Batticaloa Tigers had said that the Muslims should all be expelled by midnight. Again, the local Tigers had refused, but instead had called a meeting the next day and given them two hours' notice to leave.

A Tiger with a gun at the ready stood in front of each house as they cleared out. They were only allowed to take some clothes and one sovereign's worth of gold; the rest of their jewellery was taken off them, and body searches were conducted to make sure they weren't taking anything away. The women obviously felt humiliated and very angry at the way they had been treated – and this, too, after all they had done for the Tigers! During the IPKF occupation, the Tigers would take shelter in their houses; when the IPKF came searching, a woman would come out with a sari draped over her head and smile demurely, they would see she was a Muslim and go away, thinking that Tigers couldn't be hiding in a Muslim house.

They were all emphatic that they had never had any problems with local Tamils, had never felt persecuted or discriminated against, but had lived with them in friendship; in fact, their Tamil neighbours had come out to protest against their expulsion, but the Tigers hadn't listened to them. Now they were afraid to go back, and felt that they would be at risk while even one Tiger remained; whether they got Eelam or not, the Tigers would treat all Muslims as slaves or second-class citizens. Now their trust had been destroyed, and they would always be afraid that the same thing could happen again.

There was equal anger and bitterness over conditions in the camp, the rotten food they were given, the absence of meat, their inability to celebrate their own festivals, etc. They felt the government was not serious about helping them; even the Muslim organisation which was helping them was giving very inadequate assistance, but they didn't want to offend them by complaining. They were very much in favour of the idea that their plight should be publicised; the general feeling was that they had been forgotten, ignored, deprived of a voice. A young woman who had joined the group summed it up by saying, 'They should have killed us – even that would have been better than what we are suffering now.'

In another camp, in which the occupants had all come from Mannar island, we talked to a group of women with children. The women told us that the ultimatum to them to leave had been brought from Tigers who had come from outside. At first the local Tigers had objected, saying, 'How can we do this to people who have been feeding and sheltering us?' But ultimately they had agreed to it, going around the streets in a van with a loudspeaker telling the Muslim residents to leave within five days, and threatening to kill them otherwise.

We asked whether they were sure these were Tigers, since some Tamils in Colombo had said it was actually the government trying to clear Muslims out of the North for their own reasons. 'Most certainly they were Tigers,' said a teacher, who did most of the talking. 'Some of them were my own former pupils – there's no way I could be mistaken about them!' She had taught in a Muslim boys' school, but non-Muslim Tamil boys had also come there because the two communities were so close. Some of the Tigers who had come from outside were very young and barely literate – they had trouble reading out the lists of what people might and might not take with them. What they were allowed to take was very little: a few thousand rupees, the jewellery and clothes they were wearing, and a few other things. The rest of their things had to be left behind, although some of the local Tigers had been fairly lenient about checking and had allowed them to take more than their 'quota'. Others, however, had already started looting the Muslim families.

Their Tamil neighbours, meanwhile, had been utterly devastated by what was happening; they had literally wept, and begged and pleaded with the Tigers not to do this, but to no avail. This woman was very emphatic that there had been absolutely no enmity or hostility between the communities; on the contrary, they had lived in such close friendship – she demonstrated with hands clasped together – that if a family in one community was having a wedding and couldn't afford all the expenses, a neighbour in the other community would even sell jewellery in order to help out: so close were they, she said, like brothers and sisters.

When they left, many of them had left valuables with Tamil neighbours, thinking that even if they themselves could not return, at least their friends could enjoy the use of these articles. But their Tamil friends had wailed, 'What will happen to us once you are gone?', reckoning that the presence of the Muslims had acted as some kind of restraint on the armed forces, but that once they were gone, the remaining residents would be subjected to merciless bombardment. (Another informant said that this fear had led to a simultaneous exodus of Tamils.)

Since the Tigers had already blown up the causeway linking Mannar island to the mainland, the Muslim refugees were trapped, with no alternative but to travel to the mainland by fishing boat. Many of them waited up to five days on the beach in the pouring monsoon rain, waiting for a boat to take them across. And these were people in all conditions – old, young, sick, pregnant. One old person and one child had fallen in the water and drowned. One woman gave birth to a baby; she survived, but the baby died and had to be buried when they reached the camp. Those who had been residents of Mannar town had already been displaced some months earlier to villages outside, due to the aerial bombing and shelling by the Sri Lankan forces, in which many people had been wounded, had lost arms and legs and in some cases their lives. We were not told what happened to the injured people, but there didn't seem to be any of them in the camp, nor did it seem likely that they could have undertaken such a journey in their condition.

The women said that exposure to the wind and rain had torn much of their clothing to shreds; they felt especially bad that their children, whom they had cared for with so much trouble, had been exposed to all this while they were helpless to do anything about it. Even some of the few belongings they had managed to salvage had to be thrown away in the desperate flight: where it was a choice between people and luggage, people obviously got priority. The fishing boat owners too wanted to get what they could out of the situation, charging 6,000 rupees per family to take them across. Not everyone could afford this, so some included those who couldn't afford it as part of their 'family'. Fishing boats meant to carry five or six people were loaded with up to 40 people; one woman said she was convinced their last moment had come when their boat, its edge just two inches above the water, threatened to capsize; and yet, thanks to God's protection, they had managed to survive and reach the shore safely.

The whole experience sounded like a dreadful nightmare, and the women were baffled and hurt by the way they had been treated. One said, 'When they started looting us it was bad enough, but then we thought they would leave us alone. We never expected them to do this! Why did they have to do this to us? If they had been good to us, we would have supported them.'

What was impressive, however, was that at no point did they blame ordinary Tamils for what the Tigers had done to them; in this they were unlike the majority of Sinhalese refugees, and confirmed once again the impression that the latter had been confused and misled by anti-Tamil propaganda. Everything the Muslim refugees said, both in Puttalam and in Colombo, conveyed a picture of a closely integrated, multi-ethnic community without any ethnic or religious tensions.

If Sinhalese and Muslims have suffered, however, the worst victims of the struggle for Tamil Eelam have in some ways been the Tamils themselves. I have already mentioned two Tamil refugees with Sinhalese husbands, one in a Tamil and one in a Sinhalese camp; the young man who showed us round one of the Tamil camps had a Sinhalese father and Tamil mother (both in Jaffna), a large number of people in the Tamil camps could speak Sinhala, and vice versa. With all these indications of close links between the communities, one might expect appalling tragedy if attempts are made to tear them apart, and this is precisely what I found.

In one of the Tamil camps, I met two sisters from Batticaloa. The elder sister had been working in the Fisheries Corporation when she met her future husband, a Sinhalese fisherman. They fell in love, managed to overcome opposition from both families, and got married. Then her younger sister and her husband's younger brother also fell in love and secretly got married, much to the disgust of their families, and a third sister too married a Sinhalese man. Their children were all Sinhala-speaking. When the war broke out in June, the families, fearing for the safety of the men, sent them ahead to Colombo. Some time later the women and children followed, and at the refugee camp met someone who had been on the same bus as their menfolk. Apparently it had been stopped by the Tigers, who had taken out the Sinhalese passengers and killed them: not even shot them, but hacked them to death.

'We haven't told the children what happened to their fathers – how can we explain to them?' said the eldest sister. 'But my eldest daughter is eight years old, she understands everything. I have to tell her to keep away when we talk like this, otherwise she listens and asks questions.' Indeed, one of the children, smiling innocently, told me, 'My father has gone to the village.' The second sister was in her ninth month of pregnancy, and no arrangements seemed to have been made to take her to hospital for the birth of her baby. The eldest could operate a sewing machine, and wanted a job in a garment factory so that she could earn and support the others in Colombo. 'We can't go back,' she said, 'we will be looked on with suspicion because our children speak Sinhala. Nor can we go and stay in our husbands' family's village. I stayed there for three years, but now we can't go back because they got so angry about the second marriage!'

A Tamil schoolgirl who had been studying in the Sinhala medium told me how her education had been interrupted yet again six months after she had settled down in Batticaloa as a refugee:

> • For six months I went to school; then the Tigers came and cut and killed my teachers – Sinhala teachers. And broke the school. My science teacher, they cut and killed her.

Even women teachers!

Yes. And my home science teacher – they shot her.

Did you like your teachers?

Oh yes, my teachers were very good!

So since '87, you haven't properly been to school?

No, no, no. I'm trying to study now – my mother is teaching me.

Her mother told me:

> • In Batticaloa the Tigers wanted to kill me because they said I was Sinhalese. You see, I speak Sinhala better than Tamil because I studied in the Sinhala medium in Anuradhapura. Then they looked at my daughter, she also studied in the Sinhala medium, so they said this is a Sinhalese woman married to a Tamil and we must kill her. I pleaded with them that I was not Sinhalese, I said I could show them my birth certificate to prove I was Tamil. Then they went away. My husband got harassed too. He's a mechanic, he repairs whatever is brought to him, but the Tigers would accuse him of repairing bicycles for the army, the army would accuse him of repairing bicycles for the Tigers, and both would threaten him. In Colombo, they wanted to kill us because we are Tamil; in Batticaloa, they wanted to kill me because they said I was Sinhalese. There is no freedom anywhere in this country!

The observation that ethnic nationalism, whether Sinhalese or Tamil, involves a denial of personal freedom, was echoed by a Sinhalese refugee:

> • Look at the situation of all those families where mixed marriages have taken place. Can a husband leave his wife? Or can a woman leave her husband? Can the parents leave their children? No, they can't. And yet it has become very difficult for them to live together. Both communities look on them with suspicion. They can't find any place to live together in peace. There is no freedom in this country anywhere! And what about the Tamil families who are Sinhala-speaking? They too face the same problem. Tamils look on them with suspicion because they are Sinhala-speaking; Sinhalese look on them with suspicion because they are Tamil. Where can they go? There is no freedom anywhere.

What she and others are pointing out is that Sri Lanka has developed historically as a multi-ethnic nation in which different communities are inextricably mixed; attempting to split up its territory on an ethnic basis is a process as violent and bloody as tearing a human being limb from limb. No one can expect the victim to survive such an operation. The establishment of a Tamil nation in the North and East will be as much of a restriction on the freedom of Tamils as on that of other communities. Large numbers of people like me, whose family home has always been in the South, will have to get visas in order to live at home – which is surely an absurd situation! As Sri Lankans, we have enough difficulties getting visas to other countries; why should we add to our problems by voluntarily excluding ourselves from the greater part of our own country?

Just as the Sinhalese have suffered from the policies of their nationalists, the Tamils too have suffered the devastating impact of the violence within their own community. It is a tragic irony that a struggle which purportedly started partly because Tamils were being denied higher education should end by destroying even the existing higher education facilities and opportunities for development in the predominantly Tamil areas. For example, the attitude of the LTTE to the Eastern University in Batticaloa has hardly contributed to its survival as an institution of higher education:

> Towards the end of August the transformers supplying electricity to the university were blasted... For the university as an institution catering for the development of the region, the loss of electric supply meant a significant loss. The university's Department of Agriculture was involved in a project to find organic alternatives to weedicides. They had been collecting and storing varieties of fungi with the aim of culturing ones that would attack weeds in rice fields while not harming the rice. Equipment had been provided by British overseas development aid worth 10,000 pounds. Without electricity all this effort of storing went waste...
>
> On 27th September the Tigers abducted the university registrar for a so-called inquiry (later released) and about the same time told the inmates of the camp that they must vacate by the 1st October... The discipline that had held all this time suddenly broke down. The community that was coming together disintegrated. The people, together with the LTTE, started stripping the university. The LTTE brought bullock carts. People took away things which meant nothing to them – chemical balances, micro computers, video screens etc. These gadgets and university furniture started appearing all over the surrounding area (UTHR (Jaffna) Report No.7, Chapter 4).

Not only higher education, but even school education has been disrupted as younger and younger children have been pressed into the fighting forces. As in 'Sinhala Buddhist' Sri Lanka, apparently the only career open to the youth of Tamil Eelam is that of killing:

> We have observed that during the current situation, a large number of young persons are joining the LTTE… Many of the boys joining are about the age of 12… The young recruits are sent into action after rudimentary training lasting about two weeks and are often sent for frontline duty. It is said that the casualty figures from this group are not reflected in official lists of martyrs… As the result of frontline positions being most prone to bombing and shelling, a number of very young persons have been maimed with limbs lost (UTHR (Jaffna) Report No.5, Chapter 4).

Having once joined, with very little idea of what is involved, these children are trapped. Here is an account of their plight based on the testimony of teenagers who had succeeded in leaving the movement:

> After a couple of days inside, the initial allure had gone, life inside was oppressive and many of them wanted to leave. One of the children told the man in charge that he wanted to go home. Immediately, everyone was called together and he who wanted to go home was given a sound public thrashing. The others who also wanted to go then kept quiet. Their parents who succeeded in tracing them came to the camp and asked for their children. Each child was faced with his parents and asked if he wished to go home. The answer was consistently 'no'. In due course a few were given drugs that made them feel violent. They were given the freedom to let loose by torturing prisoners…
>
> Another revealing instance is that of a young girl from Karaveddy who joined the LTTE… During the Jaffna Fort operation last year, the mother received a letter smuggled out of a camp by a labourer. The letter from her daughter said that she was in Nelliady girls' camp and desperately wanted to go home… The mother went to the camp with a friend to plead her case. The leader of the camp repeatedly denied the girl's presence. In desperation, the mother produced her daughter's letter. The leader read the letter, called out the girl, and in her mother's presence slapped her and kicked her with her boot. She then sent the mother away telling her that her daughter will never be released (UTHR (Jaffna) Report No. 8, Chapter 5).

The torture and killing of Sinhalese by Sinhalese, which occurred in the course of the struggle for state power during the JVP uprising, was mirrored by the internecine fighting between Tamil militant groups, with the LTTE, which emerged victorious, playing the role of the Tamil state torturing and killing its Tamil victims:

> Although the Tigers had banned the other organisations after killing large numbers of their cadre, there were some who were able to escape from them. The process of hunting the remaining cadre is still going on. Those who get caught by the LTTE are being tortured brutally in order to get internal information about the movement to which they had earlier belonged. After the IPKF withdrawal, i.e. with the commencement of peace negotiations with the Sri Lankan government, the arrests had been on the increase. Some boys who sought refuge in Colombo were taken to Jaffna with the connivance of the Sri Lankan security forces, on the basis that they belonged to certain movements which were banned earlier by the LTTE. Similarly the prisoners from Jaffna were taken to the famous camp in Thunnukai, passing the Elephant Pass camp which was manned by the Sri Lankan forces. The estimates of the number of prisoners now in captivity under the Tigers range from 2,000 to 6,000. More reliable estimates put the number between 3,000 to 4,000. The brutal manner in which the LTTE torture their prisoners in underground bunkers, using boys often below the age of 16 as torturers, brings out the true colour of the struggle. The sadistic and dastardly depths to which children who 'volunteer' their services are broken and depraved by the LTTE is a comment on the liberation it offers to the community... (UTHR (Jaffna) Report No. 9, Chapter 3).

Reproduced below are some excerpts from the affidavit of an escapee to highlight the gruesome reality which prevails in Tiger prisons:

> "There is a bed made of a cement slab which is kept in a slanted position. Its width is 4ft and length 7ft. There is a chain fixed on to it permanently. Each prisoner is made to sleep with his head downwards and the legs upwards while he is chained. This awkward posture reminds me of Jesus Christ on the cross. The prisoner's chest is also tightened by a belt. Apart from the head, no other part of the body can be moved. Then the face is covered with a thick towel. An LTTE boy holds down both sides of the towel with his legs and pours water on the face. At this point the prisoner can't breathe and he screams. He is asked to tell the truth, and they insist on

confirming their allegations. If anybody is adamant, they will keep on pouring water…

Keeping the prisoner in the same position they will roll a wooden roller with an iron bar inserted in it from top to bottom all over the body. The roller may weigh about 300 lbs. When they do that, bones will crack and the skin of the body will peel off.

There is a room, very small in size, like a tiny toilet, even without ventilation holes. They will leave the prisoner in that room and send smoke from burning chilies inside. If they do not answer, this will continue. The prisoner, who is fully naked, starts to cough and sometimes bleeds…" (UTHR (Jaffna) Report No. 9, Chapter 3).

And so it goes on. The suppression of criticism and dissent, symbolised in the 'Sinhala Buddhist' nation by the killing of Richard de Zoysa, has its parallels in the Tamil nation too, the most celebrated case being the LTTE's murder of lecturer, feminist and human rights activist Rajani Thiranagama. Not merely open criticism, but any sign of independent thinking is immediately crushed:

On the 26th August 1991, students Manohar and Chelvi were arrested by the LTTE… Manohar, who was grieved by the rampant violence which had enveloped our community, was angry about the role played by intellectuals in the university and expressed his opinions very openly. He was very much involved in all the activities of the university students and tried his best to keep his independence. This was too much for the LTTE 'policemen' in the university to bear…

The LTTE has not given any reason for Chelvi's arrest. But she was arrested the day before the public staging of a drama in which she was to act… The drama was basically about a Palestinian prisoner who was tortured by the Israelis… No one thought it would offend the LTTE. It occurred to people only much later that although torture and mistreatment of prisoners by state powers had been experienced by many Tamils, this experience was at the time alien to the LTTE. Its cadre had been ordered to take cyanide as a means of evading capture… To the LTTE, torture and brutality towards prisoners were not things experienced by themselves but only what they notoriously mete out to others. And worse, a member of the Jaffna literary scene, now working for the LTTE, had commented that the heroine in the play was strongly reminiscent of the late Dr Rajani Thiranagama. (UTHR (Jaffna) Report No. 9, Chapter 5).

Finally, not even their own members were immune from repression by the Tamil nationalist groups:

> Due to internecine strife between the groups and internal repression, for which LTTE, PLOTE [People's Liberation Organisation of Tamil Eelam] and TELO were famous, a large number of cadre were killed, many of them without seeing action against Sri Lankan forces…
>
> The following facts about the long rumoured 'Green Boat' came to light after certain top ranking members left the movement. This would explain much about the character of the LTTE. During the training period in India the cadre were monitored intensively. The cadre who had the potential to decide what was right and wrong on their own, and who had a rebellious tendency to think and act by themselves, were identified or marked as a potential threat to the movement. After finishing the training, all the trained cadre were sent to the North and East of Sri Lanka in several boats. Those who had been identified or marked as a 'potential threat' were made to travel in the 'green boat'. Those who embarked on the 'green boat ride' never reached the other earthly shore. In mid sea their destiny was decided. After killing them, the bodies with the stomachs slit open were thrown into the brine – a trick with which the Sri Lankan forces are said to have become adept during the 14 months they were chums with the LTTE. Bodies so treated sank without the embarrassment of turning up on shores (UTHR (Jaffna) Report No. 9, Chapter 3, p. 12).

These accounts corroborate and expand on the stories of Tamil refugees, in Britain as well as Sri Lanka, who are fleeing the LTTE or other Tamil groups. They suggest very strongly that Eelam is not the solution to the problems of ordinary Tamils, but simply makes their lives even harder. Nor, I feel, is it the solution most Tamils would choose, if they were given real freedom of choice. There are Tamils who feel that open discussion of the ugly side of Tamil nationalism is a disservice to the 'Tamil cause'; but for most Tamils I talked to, the 'Tamil cause' was identified with freedom from discrimination and persecution rather than the establishment of a totalitarian Tamil state.

Perhaps some Tamils may feel it is worth fighting and dying for a Tamil state in which they will be tortured by Tamil rather than Sinhalese torturers, but to most Tamils the language spoken by the torturer is immaterial. Tamils in a position of safety who wilfully close their eyes to the atrocities of the militants bear part of the responsibility for the continuing destruction of the

Tamil community in Sri Lanka. It has to be acknowledged openly and honestly that the 'cause' of the Eelamists is not the same as the 'cause' of the Tamil people, and just as leading Zionists were willing to sacrifice millions of Jews to the 'cause' of a Jewish state (see Schoenman 1988, Ch. 6), so the Eelamists have shown themselves willing to sacrifice most of the Tamil population of Sri Lanka to the 'cause' of a Tamil state.

The perception of ordinary Tamils in Sri Lanka, crushed between Sinhalese and Tamil nationalism in much the same way that Sinhalese villagers found themselves crushed between the government and the JVP, was expressed very vividly by a traveller on his way north to visit his family in Jaffna. After having characterised the current Sri Lankan regime as being 'worse than that of Idi Amin,' and the policy of the Buddhist clergy as being 'Sunday sil, Monday kill' (sil = prayers), he told me confidentially, 'But the idiom of the Tigers is "brothers".'

'What does that mean?' I asked, mystified.

'Premadasa is the big brother, Prabhakaran is the younger brother: they are both exactly the same.' Then, indicating the young Sinhalese soldier in battle-dress patrolling the railway carriage, 'The Tigers also look like them and behave like them. They're exactly the same – you can't tell the difference.'

For this man, as for many others, Tamil 'identity' had very little to do with ethnicity. Discussing my mixed parentage, the fact that I was educated in Sinhala rather than Tamil and cannot claim to be Tamil in any cultural sense, I happened to mention that my family had been displaced in the 1958 riots. 'Then you are Tamil,' he said decisively, as though that settled the matter, implying that it is a history of persecution, rather than anything else, which defines Tamils as Tamils in Sri Lanka.

It seems that ethnic nationalism, whether of the 'Sinhala Buddhist' or Tamil variety, does not stop at denying the rights of people of other communities, but goes on to deny the rights even of its own people. Perhaps in an ideology and set-up where some people have the power to deny the rights of others, it is only in this negative way that the essential unity of the human race can be asserted: their unity in oppression. In any case, if Sinhalese nationalism has been the cause of all the problems, it seems illogical to conclude that a similar form of nationalism can be the solution; nor did most of the Tamil refugees I interviewed draw this illogical conclusion. If one ethnic nationalism causes the problem, two can only compound it. The solution has to be something completely different.

Chapter 7: The only solution: a homeland for all

If Eelam is not the solution to the conflict in Sri Lanka that is causing the refugee problem, what is? When I asked the Tamil refugees what the prospects were for improvement, they had intelligent and constructive answers:

• I think both Tamils and Sinhalese must get together and regard themselves as Sri Lankans, instead of saying 'Tamils', 'Sinhalese', 'JVP', 'Tigers', this, that and the other. All Sri Lankans must regard themselves as Sri Lankans… I think the problem can be solved if there's a good leader who is sincere and who wants to bring about peace in Sri Lanka. What we lack is good leaders.

• We need a better understanding between the two communities. I think we must create a better understanding by talking, by negotiating, by a give-and-take attitude… [My relationship with Sinhalese] is very friendly, cordial and understanding. As people they are very nice, as friends they are good; but when the issue of Tamil comes up, I don't know how they react. As friends they are good to me; and especially when there is trouble, like the riots, some of my friends helped Tamils even without knowing them.

On the other hand, I have some other friends, they are good to me, but when there is some problem, they are very bad to Tamils. There are even some people who are friends when the situation is normal, but when it becomes abnormal, they are hostile even to us – hostile to their own friends.

• I don't think you can predict [positive change] for at least another ten years. Because people have to get over those feelings, both the Sinhalese and the Tamils. So it takes time. Only time will heal their wounds. Till then, I don't think they will come to a settlement. That is my opinion.

The government should change their policies first… They must give equal chances. You can't go and say for education also it should be according to population! They were not giving credit for intelligence. Earlier, intelligent people were able to get into university, and the university crowd was good. Now it's not like that: anyone can get in. [It should be] on merit. You must give credit for that. You mustn't look to see whether the person is a Muslim or Tamil, you must give credit to the person.

• They must come to the negotiating table without any demands – everyone, every militant group, including the JVP.

• They must come to the table to talk, without demanding anything – I mean, without putting conditions. Everyone must have only one mind: Sri Lanka wants peace, the Sri Lankan people want a peaceful life. And then negotiate on that basis. Most people want peace now. Every year, nearly 6,000 students go to university. But during the last seven or eight years, no one has passed out. So nearly 50,000 students couldn't pass their exams – their education has come to a stop. Everything has come to a stop in the North.

Is it possible for Sinhalese and Tamils to live in harmony?

Yes. It is possible if everyone is taught both languages – Sinhala and Tamil. Because communication is very important. If I want to express my opinion to Sinhalese people and I don't know Sinhala, I can't. If I get a translator, he is never going to express exactly my feelings. (This refugee was a victim of torture by the Sri Lankan security forces.)

• The movement is changing now, but I think if the government gave equal rights to Sinhala and Tamil people, they would accept it. I think the Sinhalese have changed their minds now. Earlier there was racism; political party members told them, 'Tamil bastards, hit them,' and anything they were told, they would believe it and do it. But now I think most of the Sinhalese have changed their minds – I think so. Now they don't believe the political leaders.

• Everyone should give up their weapons without making conditions and come to the negotiating table, including the Sri Lankan forces. [The Sinhalese] haven't got a proper leader! If they have a good leader without racist ideas, they could live together.

• I think the government should negotiate with the Tigers and the JVP, and I would like both Tamil people and Sinhalese people to get freedom.

Do you think Sinhalese and Tamil people can live side by side?

That was an earlier problem, wasn't it? Now the Sinhalese and Tamils are in the same situation, and maybe they will sort out the problems okay, if they get freedom and everything.

• If all the boys are cooperative, then there will be a positive change: not otherwise. If they join together, if there is no selfishness… If they are freedom fighters, their motive should be to free Tamils from Sinhalese harassment and everything. For that, they must cooperate, they must combine together. Now they are fighting among themselves. They should get together.

[The Sinhalese] are good people by nature. Only the political situation changes their minds. Generally, there are only very small differences between the Tamils and Sinhalese.

• It's not an impossibility [to live together peacefully], and if we try hard enough it can be done. Of course now, after '83, it has become much more difficult. But I don't say it's impossible – it is possible.

• The groups have to join together in one, and then have some sort of professional politicians – people with real knowledge of the problem – to put forward a solution.

Do you think it's possible to live together peacefully?

• I think it's possible, but… I think both sides must make the effort. I don't think it's got something to do with anything personal – it's more than that. At the top level it has to be corrected. I think it's not between just an ordinary Tamil family and an ordinary Sinhalese family. It's at the political level.

Some of the refugees, feeling that the warring parties on both sides would not come to a settlement and stop fighting even if there was understanding between the communities, felt the need for intervention from outside which was genuinely neutral, unlike, in their view, the Indian government's intervention:

• There is one and only one hope that I have, which is that international peace-keeping forces are involved… in which case, all parties might have to give in. So long as it is not Indian and not Tamil… So if you get somebody from outside who is seen as being neutral…

Some Sinhalese just don't want the United Nations Peace-Keeping Force to come in – because if they come in, they will probably insist on some human rights of the Tamils. And they won't like it.

• I think India and Sri Lanka must ask the boys to return their weapons – that's the democratic way. Disarm all boys… (But) they won't. Unfortunately, the Sri Lankan government is giving arms to the Tigers. [At the time I couldn't believe this, but it subsequently became common knowledge and was even admitted by the government that they were supplying the Tigers with arms during the period of the ceasefire/talks – arms which were turned against the Sri Lankan forces and possibly also Sinhalese and Muslim civilians once the IPKF had left.] Then, automatically the Indian army will supply arms to the other groups. Then both of them will start to fight.

So do you think any other political solution is possible?

I think now the international links… the other governments must advise the Sri Lankan government to make a peaceful solution. Because now everyone is on a power struggle, and for the power struggle they are doing mad, mad things. I think good political advice is very essential to the Sri Lankan government – and to the groups, because even last month they have killed a very popular Tamil leader [Amirthalingam, leader of the TULF]. Because they went to [his] home for a negotiation talk.

In general, how would you describe your relationships with Sinhalese people?

I think, when you compare, after going round the world and seeing other people's areas and cultures and everything, Sri Lanka is one of the best countries naturally and culturally – even the community there. If the politicians stop using the press for religious and language propaganda, if they allow the people to live peacefully, they will do it.

• This government, in my view, is an illegitimate government, primarily because the constitution of 1978 was not mandated by the people. It introduced an executive presidency where the president had all power in his hands – certainly not with the consent of the people. Then the 1982 referendum was rigged to such an extent that they were able to show 51 per cent voting for the government, which is utter rubbish. Then the presidential election of 1982 was also manipulated by the government. So that today, we have had elections again to parliament after a lapse of more than 11 years; and even these parliamentary elections were manipulated by the government – there have been criticisms of it by Lord Avebury, who is the chairman of the Parliamentary Human Rights Group.

Now, my thesis is this: the whole thing must be completely dissolved; first of all it is necessary for an international body like the ICRC to go in, to trace missing persons – disappearances – and look at the treatment of detainees in the various army camps and prisons; and another international body, preferably under the UN, to move in, disarm all groups, have fresh elections, so that the elected representatives will draft a new democratic constitution where power will be returned to the people – and when we say 'people', we mean *all* the people!

All the parties – meaning, the people who have suffered – should participate in any agreement – people who really face the problems, not the people who are living here in Britain or in Canada; people in Sri Lanka itself, they should participate in any settlement – their representatives, real representatives, not the puppets appointed by the Indian government or any other government. And free elections should be held under the supervision of an international body – fair elections should take place. And the youth should be given a proper place in the government machinery.

Have you had Sinhalese friends in Sri Lanka, or Britain?

Mostly in Sri Lanka; in Britain, one or two. I was the president of the Human Rights Organisation – HRO – in Trincomalee, so due to that I had plenty of Sinhalese friends – we got together and fought for human rights. I used to go to the district Police Superintendent if anything went wrong – not by myself but with my Sinhalese friends, all of us used to go and sort out things. We didn't want any communal riots, so we tried to settle the problems then and there. We managed to control the situation. But the '83 riot was pre-planned by the government and super-powers, no? So we were unable to do anything.

How would you describe your relationship with the Sinhalese?

I like them… I love them – that's how I would describe it.
(This refugee was a victim of severe and prolonged torture by the Sri Lankan security forces.)

Other Tamil refugees in Britain, even though they couldn't suggest specific solutions to the conflict, were far from ruling out the possibility of Sinhalese and Tamils living together peacefully. In fact, most said they had lived happily alongside Sinhalese friends and neighbours.

Tamil refugees in the camps in Sri Lanka, too, were generally critical of the idea of dividing the country, and expressed a desire to live alongside neighbours from other communities; indeed, it was clear from their friendships and intermarriages that many of them did not even categorise people in terms of their ethnicity.

> • I was studying in the Sinhala medium… My mother also studied in Sinhala. She's from Anuradhapura, and that's a Sinhala-speaking area.

What language do you speak at home?

> Before 1983, we used to talk in Sinhala. After '83, we started to talk Tamil.

Up to '83, you didn't think much about being Tamil?

> No, no. Even now I don't think in that way!

> • I don't want any 'Eelam'! I think people of different communities can live together; what we need is peace, not Eelam. I don't even think of people in terms of Sinhalese or Tamil; I don't think any community is better or worse than any other. What makes people good or bad is not the community they come from but the way they have been brought up – whether they have been taught not to beat people, not to steal, to be honest, to be truthful – the truth is very important. This has to be taught not only to children but even to grown-ups!

In a group discussion, where one woman expressed somewhat sectarian sentiments – e.g. seemed to be blaming all Muslims and Sinhalese for what the Home Guards and security forces had done – others took issue with her, and she finally agreed that attacking innocent people was no solution to the problem:

• I'm glad the Muslims have been expelled from the North, because they have chased us out of our homes.

• But not all Muslims are like that – only the Home Guards are a problem. We have very good Muslim friends – in fact, we left our house in their care when we had to leave.

• I still think it's difficult to live together now, because people on both sides have lost relatives, there is a desire for revenge – I think the Muslims and Sinhalese also feel the same. Even if there is peace, we can't forget the people who have been killed. For example, in Batticaloa, one mother hid her three children in a room, and told the security forces no one was there. They started to go, but then they heard the children laughing and came back, and despite the mother prostrating herself at their feet, they killed all three children in front of her eyes. How can people forget such things, even if there is peace? The pain and bitterness will always remain. Because it was a woman, she couldn't do anything. But if it had been a man who saw his three brothers killed in front of his eyes, surely he would want to take revenge by killing someone too!

It's true that people who have committed such atrocities should be punished, but what is the point of attacking innocent people?

• When armed groups are fighting, ordinary people are suffering.

• It's wrong to hurt innocent people. Both sides are wrong.

• Yes, that's true. Killing innocent people only makes things worse.

• Now in practice there's a separate state in the North, only there's no development – everything is made from palmyra! [general laughter]. I don't want to go back to Jaffna unless there is peace – things are terribly expensive, we would be questioned, money would be extorted from us, and all that kind of thing.

• I was living in Anuradhapura during the 1983 riots, and we took shelter with Sinhalese friends. They kept us for a week, and gave us food and shelter.

- They should stop fighting and talk, solve the problems by discussion.

- I would like all three communities to live together in peace.

- Yes, that's right [general agreement].

These are not the words of fanatics ready to endorse any atrocity in order to achieve Tamil Eelam. On the contrary, they are calling for an end to the power struggle between rival Tamil groups; a stop to the fighting; negotiations, dialogue, communication, mutual understanding; equal rights and equal opportunities; a common struggle for freedom and human rights.

So far as demands on the Sri Lankan government are concerned – an end to human rights violations and colonisation schemes based on massacring and driving out Tamils, and equal rights and opportunities for minorities – granting them is a matter of simple justice; it can be done unilaterally, without any need for negotiations with anyone. Such a move would, I believe, do more to defeat the separatist struggle than all the military victories in the world.

There is no sense that these refugees regard all or even the majority of Sinhalese people as enemies; the predominant feeling is a preference for inter-ethnic friendship rather than separatism. However, in other cases there was also a recognition that the past puts obstacles in the way of their preferred solution. Many of the refugees had suggestions for ways in which these obstacles could be overcome, and foremost among these were proposals for devolution, autonomy or federalism:

Are you in favour of a federal solution?

- If it is a fully-fledged federal government, yes. If there's no discrimination, and if that's guaranteed, I think we will accept a federal government.

  The devolution of powers must be practical, or rather comprehensive and constructive, so that Tamils may feel secure. So that what happened may not be repeated – at least they don't want another July 1983.

What are the prospects for a positive change in the future?

Unless Mr Premadasa himself comes down and gives Tamils their rights in the North and East – that is part of it, he must give the rights to their way of taking things up, like having Tamil as a national language, using it in the kachcheri [government office] and so forth: these people have their Sinhalese, so why not? – unless things like that come, nobody can guarantee better things in the future.

Have you had any Sinhalese friends, colleagues or neighbours?

My mother has been the secretary of the Sri Lanka Women's Association, so she's involved with the Sinhalese. Some Tamils think, 'Why should she move with the Sinhalese?' But back in Sri Lanka we were all living together, we were neighbours, we had such a nice friendship with them. So we don't think they are our enemies.

• For me, I am from Batticaloa, you know; from 1956 I had so many bad experiences from the Sinhalese people and the Sinhalese army. But up to 1983, there was very much less suffering for the Jaffna people. In a way – educationally and job-wise – they were suffering; but Batticaloa people, they suffered a lot... attacks and all these things. Violence.
   My final solution – that is my opinion – is that we should have... not a separate country, but separate ruling and... a federal state with some autonomy... Because I can't say the Sinhalese are all enemies and all that – there are good people, there are good people, you know...
   In Sri Lanka, when we were working, for most of the time – about 13 years out of 14 – we were living in Sinhalese areas. They helped a lot in my day-to-day life, they helped my wife and my family... The Sinhalese – generally they are very polite, very simple people. It's only the politicians who have created problems.

• I think a separate state may make it better – not a separate country, but a federal state, like in India. Now we have some more problems in the Eastern Province: now there aren't Sinhalese-Tamil riots, now it's Muslims and Tamils. Last month was the worst incident in Amparai. It has cost some lives – I heard about 130 people have been killed on both sides. Because they also have some militant group now – now they are dominating some parts of the Eastern Province.

So they won't like to be under a Tamil state?

They can't be – it's very difficult; we can't solve that problem. We can solve that problem only if we separate the Eastern from the Northern Province. If the two are joined, there will be some problems in the future – you can't say in what way it will arise. Because in the Eastern part there's a majority of Muslims, and they won't accept Tamils being over them...

Only if we get a separate state in the Eastern Province can we get some peace. If we don't get that, we'll be better off living with the Sinhalese.

• Actually the problem depends on the Sri Lankan government – the Sri Lankan government can solve it if they give Tamil people equal opportunities and equal rights, autonomous status and a federal arrangement... If they solve these problems, there is no reason to go on fighting.

• Even if they give us a separate state, I don't think that would solve the problem; again it would be separated some more! Better not to give a separate state as such. Maybe just... like in India they have... a federal state. That will be the best. And even then, I really don't know how it's going to work out. I don't think that people would like it even if the Tigers came to power and got everything... Not only the Muslims – even the Tamils! They are scared – they think these people are very rigid and violent and one-track-minded.

• We can negotiate with them – with the Sri Lankan government – to get more devolution of power... We can solve our problems if there is more devolution.

Is it possible for Sinhalese and Tamils to live side by side without conflict?

That may happen, but it would be a different set-up. After we sort out our matters, that would be a different set-up, not like this.

• [A solution would be] what was agreed by J.R. Jayawardene with Rajiv Gandhi: powers given to the Northern and Eastern Provinces; even though not a separate state, more power to rule, like in India; a federal state, like India. In India there are so many states, and they are all enjoying their rights of language. There is no problem if it's like that... Even if it is not agreed to by certain extremists, I think that may be the foremost solution, at least to calm the situation.

Have you ever had any Sinhalese friends, colleagues or neighbours?

Why not? I have plenty of good Sinhalese friends! In fact, when I was in the university, all the Tamil people had a Tamil room-mate. I was the only man having a Sinhalese room-mate all the four years. Because I was born and bred in Colombo, I had the knowledge of Sinhala. So I have a lot of Sinhalese friends all over.

• You cannot expect 100% normality or 100% rights for the Tamil people or 100% Sinhala-Tamil unity. But the only thing that should be done is to see that the Sri Lanka government doesn't go amok. There should be some guarantor, either in the form of the United Nations, or the Commonwealth – any organisation which could have control over the government of Sri Lanka. Otherwise at any time this racism could be triggered by the government; nothing else could prevent it.

What do you think would be a solution to the conflict?

A solution? That's no difficulty at all. Devolution and autonomy to the North and East, and rule out, in the constitution and in the administrative set-up, discrimination in the name of race or religion in employment and education; and make the Tamil people feel, and make them be proud, that they are Sri Lankans. And also, for them to be taken into the mainstream of Sri Lankan politics. In Sri Lanka, at present, the government is Sinhalese; the central government should be a government of the Sinhalese and Tamils. We should have a separate planning division, separately for Tamils, for land, for higher education, for employment, etc., and a similar set-up for the Sinhalese, and a central government; but equal administration should be carried out from the central government to the state or regional governments.

But now it's not so: the central government is a Sinhala government. That situation should change. Until that happens, even if there's a pact or peace formula signed or adopted between the Sri Lanka government and the Tamil minorities, you cannot expect fair play on the part of the Sri Lanka government to implement it. That's why there must be someone to guarantee. When India intervened, we thought India was going to be a guarantor. But I think India has failed in that act of being a guarantor because they have not understood the real situation.

The proposals for autonomy are a good deal more problematic than the solutions suggested earlier; they raise, for example, questions of where the boundaries of the autonomous areas should be, the degree and scope of devolution, and the protection of minority rights within each area – for example, the rights of Muslims and Sinhalese within a predominantly Tamil area. However, I feel it is worth giving serious consideration to these proposals, because they are made by people who are ready to live in peace and friendship with Sinhalese people in a united Sri Lanka, although they feel that Tamil rights and security cannot be assured unless there is some form of devolution of power.

The refugees who wanted a federal solution, along with those quoted earlier in this chapter, formed the bulk of the Tamil refugees whom I interviewed. Their freedom from communal hatred can only be described as admirable, especially when it is remembered that all of them have suffered some kind of loss, and some have suffered intensely from torture or bereavement. It appears that despite their good intentions, they have been powerless to influence events.

But perhaps it is not so. If every one of these refugees had been a fervent Eelamist, ready to do his or her utmost to bring about a separate state, if the thousands of young men fleeing recruitment had joined the fighting, what would the situation be today? I believe the carnage would have been much worse, and there would be no hope of a peaceful solution. It is the refusal of the majority of Tamil refugees, despite all they have suffered, to think in crude communal terms, which keeps that hope alive even today.

The Muslim refugees too were remarkably free of communalism in their perception of the problem. In one camp, young women said in a group discussion,

> • We don't want separate Tamil, Sinhala and Muslim states. We only want peace.

Some women in a Tamil refugee camp also said that they would like all communities to live together in peace.

> • That's not surprising – all displaced people want peace!

I asked a group of older women whether they would like to go back to their homes in the North:

> • No, now we would always be afraid we might be attacked again. We would prefer to settle down in a mixed area like Colombo.

Alongside Sinhalese and Tamil people?

• Why not? We have no problems with either Sinhalese or Tamils.

What do you think of the idea of a separate Tamil state?

• We wouldn't like to be part of it. If there were separate Sinhala, Tamil and Muslim states, we wouldn't mind.

But then there would be fighting over territory between all the groups, and the war would go on, wouldn't it?

• Yes, that's the problem.

What do you think of the idea of a single state with equality and security for people of all communities?

• [Enthusiastically] Yes, yes, we would like that.

Out of the three groups of refugees I met, it was among the Sinhalese that I came across most communalism – probably the result of relentless anti-Tamil propaganda – although in the Sinhalese camps too there were impressive examples of clear-sightedness and sanity. However, the most eloquent tribute to the basic humaneness of most Sinhalese people in Sri Lanka comes, paradoxically, in the testimony of the Tamil refugees. I have already quoted several moving accounts of assistance, solidarity and friendship. Here are a few more:

• I'll tell you a story. There was a man in our village who went to Colombo… He left Colombo on the day of the '83 violence, and he simply disappeared – for about 14 days he didn't come back. So his family performed the last rites, assuming he had been killed. Then afterwards, he was brought in by a Sinhalese. The bus had stopped 20-30 miles from Colombo on his way home, and the driver said, 'Just clear out, I can't go any further because of the violence.' This man didn't know what to do; he got down and just waited. People were being assaulted and killed and all that, and he didn't know what to do. A mob was coming for him. Then a Sinhalese man with a knife, he caught hold of this man and he said, 'Meya magé' ('This man is mine'), and took him away into the house, and kept him there in the house for 14 days, provided him with food and all that; then he took his car, put this man in, got the whole family in the car as if they were going on a trip, came to Nuwara Eliya and dropped him at home, and stayed there one or two days. So people were very happy; they collected money and offered it to them, but they refused to accept it. A lot of such incidents I have heard of. My own friends have escaped only because of help from Sinhalese friends.

• I stayed for one week in a Sinhalese house – otherwise I would have been arrested before leaving Sri Lanka.

• During the riot, some Sinhalese friends accommodated my family.

• I had a lot of friends among the Sinhalese – in fact I took shelter in a Sinhalese friend's house.

• Before I came here, I was staying with [Sinhalese friends] for three months in Colombo.

• In 1958 I was saved by [Sinhalese friends], and in '77 there were a lot of Sinhalese friends who helped us. Even in '83… as we got out of the refugee camp, we were staying with Sinhalese friends.

• I think we have more Sinhalese friends than Jaffna Tamil friends! After our house was burned, they kept us in their houses till we went to Batticaloa. In fact… one Sinhalese friend kept my husband in his house for six months, and took him to the office in his car.

• My sister and some other relatives were affected two or three times. Twice they were attacked. They have got a lot of Sinhalese friends, and every time something happens, they take shelter with the Sinhalese friends. That's the only reason they are still alive!

• I had a lot of Sinhalese friends. My husband stayed with them, and if anybody came and asked for him they would say, 'No, there's no person like him.'

So he was sheltered by them?

Yes, because they're very good friends.

• When I was in prison, I got help from my Sinhalese friends. Actually, I like Sinhalese people. During the violence in '77 or '83 or '58, some of them helped the Tamils. [This refugee was a victim of torture by the Sinhalese security forces.]

• During the troubles, when Tamils were attacked, our [Sinhalese] neighbours helped us by letting us stay with them. Even now my parents are staying with Sinhalese people.

• When I was in jail for two years between 1985 and 1987, Sinhalese friends helped me. And then at one point I was going to be shot – one person took a gun and targeted me – but a [Sinhalese] person who knew me stopped him. He was a person who was born and brought up in my area, and because of that, he saved me – not that he was a friend exactly.

Do you think it is possible in future for Sinhalese, Tamils and Muslims to live alongside each other without fighting?

Yes; if there are no arms, there will be peace. (This refugee too was a victim of torture by the Sinhalese security forces.)

• I've got plenty [of Sinhalese friends]! Actually, they have saved our lives. In '77 they helped my parents and brother, and after that, my family as a whole.

• In 1981 I was working in Kalutara District, and there was a big communal riot – they burned all the Tamil shops and everything, it happened in the upcountry areas. I was the only Tamil living in that town – I was running a clinic there. Nothing happened to me – so you can say they saved my life, I lived there just like a Sinhalese man, without any problem. A Sinhalese man, a very good friend of mine, he slept at my place and took precautions that nothing should happen to me – not only him, but all the people in the town, And the priests – the Buddhist monks – they took care, they asked me to come and stay with them in the pansala (temple). So like that, they made sure that nothing happened to me – I have to say that. Not only that time, but several times they helped me – and not only there, but in other places too.

There were other cases too of organised attempts to protect Tamils; for example, a Sinhalese civil servant in Nawalapitiya described their attempts to protect Tamils there in 1983 and 1986, and to strengthen their organisation so as to prevent riots altogether in the future.

When all these accounts and the earlier ones are put together, they provide impressive evidence of Sinhalese contributions to Tamil survival. It does not seem to have been an exaggeration when one of the Tamil refugees said that:

• If you speak to anybody who was there in Sri Lanka at that time, the estimate is that about 2,500 people were killed in the 1983 riots. If the Sinhalese people hadn't helped, the death figure would have been 50,000. Because every house has helped Tamils to escape or shelter or whatever.

Another refugee, himself a victim of severe torture by the Sri Lankan security forces, went even further:

• I used to tell our people – Tamil people who are a little communal – I used to tell them, 'If all the Sinhalese are communal, no Tamils would be left alive in Sri Lanka! So don't think like that!'

It is vitally important that this side of the story should be recorded and told – not only because it is necessary to establish the truth, but also because it shows that ordinary people, acting out of spontaneous compassion and kindness, have made a significant impact on the course of Sri Lankan history. It is thanks to the many thousands of unknown people of all communities who have resisted the poison of ethnic hatred that our recent history is not uniformly shameful. And if they have been able to shift the course of history in a positive direction in the past, they can do so in the future as well.

It is people like the majority of the refugees I interviewed, and the Sinhalese people who helped and rescued them, who can ultimately solve the problem of Sri Lankan refugees, with support and assistance from the international community, by making the whole of Sri Lanka into a genuine homeland with human and democratic rights for all its people of every ethnic community. Perhaps the first and most important step in such a process is acknowledging and publicly condemning abuses which are perpetrated in one's name. So I end with a few questions:

To the people of Britain and other Western countries: Are you going to allow your governments to continue colluding with the Sri Lankan government, which is creating refugees, while at the same time turning the refugees away when they seek asylum?

To the Sinhalese people of Sri Lanka (and abroad): Are you going to allow political parties and the security forces to continue committing atrocities in the name of Sinhala Buddhism?

To the Tamil people of Sri Lanka (and abroad): Are you going to allow militant groups to continue committing atrocities in the name of Tamil Eelam?

Consider your answers carefully, because they will go down in history!

Bibliography

Amerasinghe, Vasantha, 1989: 'Sri Lankan Presidential Election – An Analysis', *Economic and Political Weekly* Vol. 24 No.7, 18/12/89 (India).

Amnesty International, 1983-1992: Reports and Statements on Sri Lanka.

Bandaranayake, Senake, 1984: 'The Peopling of Sri Lanka: The National Question and Some Problems of History and Ethnicity', in *Ethnicity and Social Change,* ed. Social Scientists' Association (Colombo).

British Refugee Council, 1987: *Tamil Asylum Seekers: Implications for British Asylum Policy and Carrier's Liability* (London).

British Refugee Council: *Sri Lanka Bulletin and Sri Lanka Monitor* (various issues), (London).

Cohen, Steve, 1988: *From the Jews to the Tamils: Britain's mistreatment of refugees* (Manchester Law Centre, UK).

Coles, G., 1985: 'Voluntary Repatriation: A Background Study', Prepared for the Round Table on Voluntary Repatriation, UNHCR/ TIHL, San Remo, 16-19 July.

Danish Refugee Council, 1988: 'Report of a fact-finding mission to Sri Lanka undertaken by representatives of the British Refugee Council and the Danish Refugee Council from 30 July to 12 August 1988' (Copenhagen)

Danish Refugee Council, 1986: 'A Study of the Situation of the Sri Lankan Tamils in Tamil Nadu' (Copenhagen).

Danish Refugee Council, 1988: 'The Situation in Sri Lanka – An Update' (Copenhagen).

Hansen, A. and Oliver-Smith, A. (eds), 1982: *Involuntary Migration and Resettlement: The Problems and Responses of Dislocated People* (Westview Press, Colorado).

Hensman, Rohini, 2019: 'The Struggle for Democracy in Sri Lanka, *Jacobin*, 24 November. https://www.jacobinmag.com/2019/11/sri-lanka-mahinda-rajapaksa-regime

Hoole, Rajan, Daya Somasunderam, K. Sritharan and Rajani Thiranagama 1990: *The Broken Palmyra* (Sri Lanka Studies Institute, Claremont CA).

Hyndman, Patricia, 1988: *Sri Lanka: Serendipity Under Siege* (Spokesman, UK).

International Alert, 1989: *Political Killings in Southern Sri Lanka,* a compilation and report by Eduardo Marino (London).

Kismaric, Carol, 1989: *Forced Out: The Agony of the Refugee in Our Time* (Human Rights Watch and The J.M. Kaplan Fund, US and UK).

Loescher, Gil and Monahan, Laila, 1990: *Refugees and International Relations* (Clarendon Press, Oxford).

Parliamentary Human Rights Group, 1987: *Sri Lanka: A Nation Dividing* (House of Commons, London).

Perera, Janaki, 1989: *The Subversion of the Electoral Process in Sri Lanka* (no publisher or place).

Piyadasa, L., 1988: *Sri Lanka: The Unfinished Quest for Peace* (Marram Books, UK).

Samarakoen, Priya, 1988: *Sri Lanka's First Referendum: Its Conduct and Results* (Chr. Michelsen Institute, Bergen).

Schoenman, Ralph, 1988: *The Hidden History of Zionism, Chapter 6* (Veritas Press, USA).
https://www.marxists.org/history/etol/document/mideast/hidden/ch06.htm

Senewiratne, Brian, 1986: *Human Rights Violations in Sri Lanka* (Dr B Senewiratne, Australia).

Social Scientists' Association, 1984: *Ethnicity and Social Change in Sri Lanka* (Social Scientists' Association, Colombo).

Tamil Information Centre, 1986: *Militarisation in Sri Lanka,* a report compiled by Mayan Vije (London).

University Teachers for Human Rights (Jaffna), 1989–1992:
----- Special Report 1, Preface.

https://uthr.org/SpecialReports/spreport1.htm
----- Report No. 5, Chapter 2: Eastern Report.
https://uthr.org/Reports/Report5/chapter2.htm
--------------------- Chapter 4:
https://uthr.org/Reports/Report5/chapter4.htm
--------------------- Chapter 8: Jaffna Report.
https://uthr.org/Reports/Report5/chapter8.htm
--------------------- Chapter 9: Eastern Province, Southern Sector:
https://uthr.org/Reports/Report5/chapter9.htm
----- Special Report 3:
https://uthr.org/SpecialReports/spreport3.htm#_Toc15893071
----- Report No. 7, Chapter 2: https://uthr.org/Reports/Report7/chapter2.htm
--------------------- Chapter 4:
https://uthr.org/Reports/Report7/chapter4.htm
----- Report No. 8, Chapter 2:
https://uthr.org/Reports/Report8/chapter2.htm#e
--------------------- Chapter 5:
https://uthr.org/Reports/Report8/chapter5.htm
----- Report No. 9, Chapter 3: https://uthr.org/Reports/Report9/chapter3.htm
--------------------- Chapter 5:
https://uthr.org/Reports/Report9/chapter5.htm

US Committee for Refugees, 1985: *Time for Decision: Sri Lankan Tamils in the West* (USA).

US Committee for Refugees, 1987: *Sri Lankan Tamils' Search for Asylum: An Update* (USA).

Vije, Mayan, 1985: *Oppression of Tamils in Sri Lanka* (Tamil Information Centre, London).

Vije, Mayan, 1987: *Where Serfdom Thrives: The Plantation Tamils of Sri Lanka* (Tamil Information and Research Unit, UK).

Vittachi, Tarzie, 1958: *Emergency '58. The story of the Ceylon race riots* (Andre Deutsch, London).

World Alliance of YMCAs, 1987: *Emergency Appeal for Sri Lanka* (UK).